What Are They Saying About Matthew?

REVISED AND EXPANDED EDITION

Donald Senior, C.P.

PAULIST PRESS
New York/Mahwah, N.J.

Cover design by Tim McKeen.

ISBN: 0-8091-3624-4

Published by Paulist Press
997 Macarthur Boulevard
Mahwah, NJ 07430

Printed and bound in the
United States of America

Contents

Preface

To understand "what they are saying about Matthew" it is important to understand what has been said about the gospels in general in the past few decades. The post-World War II period which saw such revolutionary changes in western culture also witnessed new ways of understanding the role of the evangelists and the nature of the gospels they produced.

These new perspectives, like the broader changes in post-war society, did not appear out of thin air; they had been brewing in biblical scholarship for decades.[1] In the early part of the twentieth century, so-called "form critics" had concentrated on the period between the life of Jesus and the writing of the gospels. Their interest was on the impact of the early Christian community on the development of the gospel materials. Biblical scholars categorized the various "forms" the gospel material took because of its use and preservation in different activities or settings of the early church such as preaching, liturgy, conflicts, etc. But this focus tended to push the work of the evangelists themselves into the shadows. They were considered as mere "collectors" or editors of the gospel materials.

But a new generation of biblical scholars was not content with that conclusion. Pioneers, many of whom were German scholars, such as Willi Marxsen in his study of Mark's gospel (1956), Hans Conzelmann on the gospel of Luke (1953) and Gunther Bornkamm on Matthew (1948), recognized that the evangelists contributed much more to the present form of the gospels than merely assembling already existing materials; the evangelists brought new meaning and even content to the gospel tradition.[2] From this conviction the method of "redaction criticism" was born ("redaction" being an Anglicized version of the German word *Redaktion* or "editing").

Redaction criticism, then, focused on the contributions of the evangelist. Even though the gospel material had been preserved in the early church, the contribution of the gospel writers themselves was considerable. Not only did the evangelist assemble the contents of the gospel, but he gave this material new meaning by selecting it, putting it into an overall narrative framework, and shaping the material anew with his own perspective. Each of the four gospels is distinct because each evangelist, working in the milieu of a specific Christian community, added a new layer of interpretation to the traditions about Jesus.

Developments in gospel studies did not stop with the advent of redaction criticism, however. More recent developments in gospel studies tend to amplify and in some instances go beyond the fundamental insights of redaction criticism. One of the key convictions of redaction critics was that the evangelists not only collect and hand on traditional materials but are true authors in their own right. For that reason, some biblical scholars preferred to use the term "composition criticism" rather than "redaction criticism."[3] Before comparing and contrasting a gospel with parallel passages in other gospels, they contended, it should first be viewed as an independent whole, with its own structure and meaning.

Although the term "composition criticism" did not become a household word in biblical scholarship, the conviction that a gospel should be interpreted in the light of the entire narrative has become a dominant note of biblical studies, particularly in North America. More and more, analysts of the gospels appeal to the insights of literary criticism: if an evangelist can be considered a true author, then the dynamics and procedures that affect all literary activity should be present in the gospels and the complex and subtle literary codes within a text that convey meaning to the reader should also explain the impact of the gospels on the reader of any culture or generation.[4] The emphasis on the gospels as literature coincides with a whole new appreciation in theology and biblical studies for the power of metaphorical language and of narrative to convey religious experience. Where redaction criticism remained interested in the historical context that helped shaped a gospel, pure literary criticism suspends historical questions and focuses on the "world" created by the text itself. Put another way, one could say that historical criticism (including redaction criticism) was interested primarily in the relationship between the biblical text and the historical context that produced it, while literary criticism is interested primarily in the relationship between the text and the reader.

These distinctions are important but they should not be pressed too far. When literary criticism first came into vogue in biblical studies, some of its adherents contended that any sort of historical interest in the original milieu of a gospel or any attempt to consider the role and circumstances of the evangelist and their impact on the composition of a text compromised the integrity of a literary critical investigation of a text's meaning. But more recent studies are bringing a better balance, realizing the importance of both historical and literary vantage points. A text cannot avoid the impact of its original context, nor are the sources and intent of the author irrelevant to interpretation. By the same token, one cannot make automatic deductions about the historical context of the evangelist and his community simply by noting features within the narrative world of the gospel story and considering them direct evidence of the circumstances of the gospel community.[5]

Literary criticism has a number of derivations, such as "narrative criticism" which focuses on the dynamics and structures of the narrative, or "rhetorical criticism" which attends to the form and function of language in various literary formats, or "reader response criticism" which studies the relationship between the text and the reader. All of these methods have been employed in recent studies of Matthew, as we shall note in the pages ahead.[6]

Another recent development in gospel studies takes its cue not from literary studies but from the positive sciences. On many fronts biblical scholars have been using insights, methods and models from social sciences, such as cultural anthropology, sociology and economics, to analyze the context and impact of a New Testament work such as the gospel of Matthew. In one sense, this type of approach moves in a very different direction from that of literary criticism. Where many literary critics studiously avoid allowing assumptions about the historical circumstances of Matthew's community to affect their interpretation of his literary work, scholars using methods borrowed from the social sciences are interested not so much in the literary skill of Matthew or his theology but precisely in the first century social milieu of the evangelist and his community.

Feminist scholars have also brought important new perspectives to gospel interpretation. While a feminist approach may utilize the same methodologies we have been enumerating, an important added dimension is a critical suspicion about the androcentric bias of the biblical texts and an alertness to elements that contribute to a more inclusive perspective within the Bible. Feminist studies of Matthew are still relatively few but, as we shall see, some important work has already been done.

Each chapter that follows takes its cue from the procedures and interests of Matthean scholarship. The subjects for each chapter are not selected according to various methods or groupings of scholars but are based on issues springing from Matthew's gospel and the history of its interpretation. The first chapter concentrates on the possible milieu of Matthew's community—an important issue that has received an enormous amount of attention in the past few years as our understanding of first century Judaism and its relationship to early Christianity has been refined. The second chapter reviews the questions of what sources Matthew may have used in the composition of the gospel and what structure (or "plot") he gave his overall narrative—both questions are important leads for discovering Matthew's message. Subsequent chapters focus on major aspects of Matthew's theology: his view of salvation history, his interpretation of the Old Testament, his attitude toward the Jewish law, his Christology, and his understanding of discipleship and his theology of the church.

The reader should be aware that this list of issues is limited and, to some extent, subjective. Few scholars, I believe, would deny that these topics are major questions in Matthew's gospel; the continuing flood of articles and books under each of these headings is testimony to this. But, undoubtedly, more issues could be added to the list, such as Matthew's eschatology, his view of mission, his concern with judgment and so on. And even such an expanded list would not include the many new commentaries that have appeared in English or the numerous studies that have been published on specific passages or more confined issues within the gospel.[7] My task of accounting for recent scholarship has been simplified by the recent appearance of another book in this series. Warren Carter's *What Are They Saying About Matthew's Sermon on the Mount?* ably surveys the enormous body of literature on this portion of Matthew.[8] There is some overlap in my chapter on "Matthew's Attitude to the Law" but it is negligible and I have focused on the role of the Jewish law in the overall perspective of Matthew's gospel.

Within the limits of our book (and its author) the topics included seemed the most crucial, the most comprehensive, and the ones that can give the reader a sense of how contemporary scholarship views the gospel. Where possible, to represent a specific position I have tried to use authors whose works are available in English so that the interested reader can follow up, if he or she chooses to. And to the extent I could restrain myself, I let the authors speak for themselves, although my own evaluations and prejudices are, I'm sure, apparent in most cases.

Revising this brief volume has been a pleasant task. Going back over the fertile soil of Matthean studies reminded me how subtle and magnetic is the gospel that inspired all that scholarship. And reviewing the many books and articles that have appeared in the decade since the original edition of this book confirms the vigor of biblical scholarship and proves that new and fruitful insights are still possible. This revised and expanded edition considers more than ninety new books and articles that have appeared in the last ten years—and that is only a sampling of what has been written. Surveying Matthean scholarship has also renewed a sense of gratitude I felt toward my mentor, Frans Neirynck, professor emeritus of the University of Louvain, who first led me into the world of critical exegesis a quarter of a century ago and who himself continues to make substantial contributions to Matthean studies.

In any case, I hope that my colleagues in the biblical field and the readers whom I welcome to these pages will find here a reliable guide to what, in fact, "they are saying about Matthew's gospel."

Donald Senior, C.P.
Catholic Theological Union, March 1995

1
The Setting for Matthew's Gospel

Introduction

Like skilled preachers, the evangelists told their stories of Jesus in such a way that they would touch the concerns and hopes of their audience. And, one can assume, the issues and setting of a particular early Christian community had an impact to some degree on the evangelist and the gospel he produced. Therefore one of the major interests of biblical scholarship has been to determine the milieu of the community for which a particular gospel was written. This has certainly been the case with studies on the gospel of Matthew where, in particular, the relationship of Matthew to Judaism has been a dominant issue for scholars.

It is important to remember that practically speaking the major source for gathering information about the circumstances of Matthew's community is the gospel itself.[1] We have no direct outside information from this early period which tells us who wrote Matthew's gospel or what the problems were in his community. We do have rabbinical texts that tell us something about the situation of Judaism in the first century, but these texts were edited later than the gospels and must be used with caution when we are attempting to get a picture of this earlier period. Josephus, the famed first century historian who began as a Jewish revolutionary but ended as something of a court biographer for the Romans, provides invaluable information about the Judaism of this period but his viewpoint needs careful interpretation. Through the writings of the Christian historian Eusebius (A.D. 260-339) we also have the comments of Papias who lived in the early part of the second century, but we cannot be sure that Papias himself had solid historical information about the author of the gospel.[2]

The accumulation of recent archeological finds giving us important clues about the circumstances of life in first century Palestine, the ongoing absorption of information from the Qumran writings and more careful assessment of other non-canonical Jewish texts from this period have led to a new understanding of the diversity and complexity of first century Judaism and early Christianity. This revised viewpoint, in turn, has had an impact on the way scholars describe the relationship of Matthew and his community to his Jewish milieu.

Matthew and Pharisaic Judaism

One of the most influential studies of Matthew's milieu in recent decades was the book of W.D. Davies, *The Setting of the Sermon on the Mount*.[3] As its title indicates, this book attempted to situate the sermon on the mount in the wider context not only of Matthew's gospel but of Judaism and the early church. One of Davies' major conclusions was that Matthew's sermon on the mount and much of the rest of the gospel was formulated in direct confrontation with Pharisaic Judaism. This conclusion become an important point of reference for contemporary Matthean studies. By no means have all scholars agreed with Davies' viewpoint but the evidence he discusses and his statement of Matthew's relationship to Judaism have framed the debate.

Davies begins by reconstructing the situation of Judaism after the dramatic events of the Jewish revolt against Rome and the resulting destruction of Jerusalem and the temple in A.D. 70. Historical sources for this period are murky but the general lines of the story can be pieced together from later rabbinic traditions and from Josephus. The strongest leadership group to survive this holocaust were the Pharisees, a lay reform movement that had been only one among many groups in Judaism prior to the revolt.[4] Under the leadership of Rabbi Johannan ben Zakkai the Pharisees would be the ones to draw Jewish life out of the ashes.

Johannan was not in sympathy with the Zealot group that had led the armed revolt against Rome nor with the Essenes who had counseled complete withdrawal from the social and political scene. His more pragmatic middle course opened a way to survival. He gathered a group of scholars at Jamnia near the Mediterranean coast. Here the foundations for rabbinic Judaism would be laid. The "academy" of Jamnia offset fragmentation within Judaism by asserting the rabbis' authority as interpreters of the law and regulators of Jewish life. The village synagogue was the Pharisees' base of power. Strict observance of the law replaced the central role that the liturgical life of the temple had played in Judaism. The Jewish law would eventually be codified and the canon of Jewish scriptures formalized.

Jamnia also established a bulwark against external threats to Jewish life. Strict norms for Jewish identity were asserted to ward off the influence of pagans or of groups considered heretical. It is here, according to Davies, that Christianity came into the picture. Prior to the revolt Jewish Christians had remained within the broad boundaries of Judaism. But in the atmosphere of consolidation inaugurated by Jamnia this was no longer tolerable. The Jewish Christians, along with other groups considered heretical by the rabbis, were expelled from the synagogue. An important device for this was the insertion of the famous twelfth benediction into the Tiffilah or synagogue prayers, a reform instituted about A.D. 85. An ancient version of that prayer was discovered several years ago in the Cairo Genizah: "For persecutors let there be no hope, and the dominion of arrogance do Thou speedily root out in our days; and let Christians and *minim* (probably meaning 'heretics') perish in a moment, let them be blotted out of the book of the living and let them not be written with the righteous."[5] If any hesitated to read that prayer or to say "Amen" to it, they were liable to expulsion from the synagogue. The result was obvious. Although prior to the events of A.D. 70 the Jewish Christians had been part of Jewish liturgical and synagogue life, that was no longer possible in the atmosphere of strict identity set up by Jamnia. As Davies points out, it was not a matter of arbitrary hostility on the part of the rabbis, but a question of concern for their own identity and survival.

Davies was convinced that Matthew's gospel, especially the sermon on the mount, was "a Christian response to Jamnia" (p. 315). Matthew's church, a majority of whose members were Jewish Christians, was concerned about its own identity now that it was cut off from its Jewish roots and being absorbed into the Gentile world. Matthew, therefore, attempted to define Christian identity over against the reform of Jamnia.

In Davies' opinion evidence of this "great gulf...between the Christian community and the synagogue" (p. 286) is found throughout the gospel. Matthew refers to Jewish attacks on the report of Jesus' resurrection in 28:15. He often labels the synagogues as "their synagogues" (4:23; 9:35; 10:17; 12:9; 13:54). The "Pharisees" seem to be singled out as the group most hostile to the Matthean Jesus (5:20; 16:11-12; and especially 23:1-36).

Matthew also takes up many of the issues that were of concern to the rabbis at Jamnia. He alludes to the fall of Jerusalem (22:7) and to the infidelity of that city (23:37; 16:21; 21:10; 28:11). In the infancy narrative and in the resurrection account he seems to favor Galilee as the place of redemption instead of Jerusalem the unfaithful city, a stance that would be in opposition to that of the rabbis who were suspicious of radical movements in Galilee. The Matthean Jesus is openly critical of the ways of piety dear to the rabbis (see 6:25-34). Matthew's version of the Lord's Prayer may even be in conscious opposition to the elaborate synagogue prayer, the *Shemonah Esreh*. And, above all, Matthew's formulation of the antitheses ("You have heard it said, but I say to you"—see 5:22-48) in the sermon on the mount pits the "Torah" of Jesus against the Pharisees' interpretation of the law.

In Davies' view these and other special emphases of Matthew's gospel indicate that the evangelist formulated his gospel in a conscious dialectic with Jamnia. Matthew's community was probably located in Syria, an area which included a significant Jewish population and which was of special concern to the rabbis at Jamnia. Matthew was attempting to assist his own Christians to survive the wrenching pain of transition by clearly affirming the authority and authenticity of Jesus' own teaching and at the same time countering the attacks from the synagogue.

Matthew and Judaism: A Reassessment

Although Davies' thesis that Matthew wrote his gospel during the crucial transition phase of Judaism and early Christianity remains influential, more recent studies have offered substantial modifications. First of all, Davies may have exaggerated the singular importance of Jamnia in the reform of post-70 Judaism. As the Jewish scholar Jacob Neusner and others have pointed out, the later rabbinic traditions that speak of Jamnia tend to idealize what happened there in order to underscore the crucial role of the rabbis in later Jewish life.[6] It is unlikely that Jamnia was a formal "council" or that it had such a dominant role in Jewish life. Neusner has termed the turbulent decades that followed the destruction of the temple and the reconstitution of Jewish life as "formative Judaism"—a complex period of consolidation that only a century later would emerge as what we now call rabbinic Judaism.

Other scholars question whether Matthew and his community had actually broken with Judaism, even though conflict and tension are evidently present. Viewing Matthew as a "Christian" over against "Judaism" is, in effect, anachronistic. In a study composed at the same time as that of W.D. Davies, a German scholar, Reinhart Hummel, had championed the view that Matthew's church had not yet definitively broken with the synagogue.[7] He readily admits that Matthew's Jewish Christians were in conflict with the Pharisees, but at the time of the writing of the gospel that conflict was still an intrafamily debate. In fact, Hummel thought that Matthew was also in conflict with some Christians who were opposed to the law altogether. Thus the evangelist was fighting a war on two fronts.

Hummel finds support for his view in the gospel itself. The story about paying the temple tax in 17:24-27 is one bit of evidence. Hummel believes that Matthew writes after the destruction of the temple in A.D. 70. Even though the temple tax story stems from an earlier tradition, it still indicates that Matthew's community did not want to "scandalize" (17:27) Pharisaic Judaism. The exhortation in 23:2-3 to "practice and observe" whatever the scribes and Pharisees teach because they "sit on Moses' seat" is another indication that no definitive break with Judaism had yet occurred. Unlike Luke (6:32) and John (9:22; 12:42; 16:2) Matthew has no explicit references to exclusion from the synagogue. Warnings about persecution in the synagogues, on the other hand, imply that Matthew's church members still belonged (10:17; 23:34).

While Matthew's community is still part of the synagogue, this is an uneasy relationship. The evangelist is critical of the spirit of the Pharisees and contrasts it with Jesus' interpretation of the law which puts mercy as supreme (9:13; 12:7; 22:40). But some of the conflicts over law in the gospel reflect inner community concerns. Matthew's church is a mixed church, composed of Jews and some Gentiles, a community in contact with Greek culture. From this milieu come "Hellenistic libertines" who dismiss the law altogether. But, in Hummel's view, Matthew's church developed its own style of piety which emphasized fidelity to the law. Thus Matthew warns his church against *anomia* or "lawlessness" (see 5:17-20; 7:12-17; 11:12-13; 24:10-13). Fidelity to Jesus as messiah meant avoiding not only Pharisaic legalism but also any frivolous abandonment of the requirements of the law.

For Hummel, therefore, Matthew's community still belonged to the synagogue although the relationship was a turbulent one. At the same time, under the impact of the Jesus tradition and the influx of Gentile members, Matthew's church was developing its own style, distinct from that of Pharisaic Judaism. This independence would ultimately lead to a definitive break.

Graham Stanton, a British scholar who offers a fine survey of Matthean research in his book, *A Gospel for a New People*, follows this same line of interpretation.[8] Matthew is attempting to define his community in its relationship to Judaism in the crucial period following the Jewish war and the destruction of Judaism. Thus Matthew is one among several "sectarian" groups in Judaism involved in this kind of self-definition because of the radically different circumstances history had imposed. Stanton is less enthused about Hummel's "two-front" theory, however. He is not convinced that Matthew is dealing with an anti-law sentiment within his own community, yet he concedes that Matthew has a certain "anti-Gentile" bias. He notes, for example, the gospel's derogatory comments about Gentiles in Mt 5:47; 6:7, 32 and the expectations of suffering hostility from Gentiles in 10:18, 22. Even though committed to a mission to the Gentiles, Matthew's tightly knit community may have viewed this wider world as alien and threatening.[9]

Several recent scholars employing models from the social sciences and drawing on research about first century Palestinian Judaism have built on Hummel's perspective. J. Andrew Overman in his work, *Matthew's Gospel and Formative Judaism*, emphasizes that Judaism from the time of the Hasmonean dynasty on through the first century was a very diverse and complex reality.[10] It was characterized by various sects or factions, each of whom claimed to be faithfully Jewish and each considering their opponents and the established authority as corrupt and "lawless." Matthew's community takes its place in this sectarian landscape. The Jewish Christians of Matthew's community believed that in following the teaching of Jesus the messiah *they* were the authentic Jews and the "true Israel."[11] Yet Matthew and his community also seem to realize that their viewpoint is not the dominant one and that the Pharisaic perspective was beginning to hold sway in "formative Judaism"—thus the hostility and urgency of the gospel in attacking the Jewish leaders and claiming righteousness for those who would follow Jesus. At the same time, Matthew's community was beginning to turn its eye to the Gentile world. As yet, there were few Gentiles in the community, but the mission text that concludes the gospel (28:16-20), as well as favorable responses of Gentile characters to Jesus in Matthew's story, indicate that the future of the community may indeed lie outside of Israel.

Anthony Saldarini's work, *Matthew's Christian-Jewish Community*, may be the most emphatic in its conviction that Matthew writes from within, not outside, the Jewish community.[12] He makes full use of sociological tools to understand the relationship of Matthew's community to the wider Jewish context. Matthew's assumptions, his language, the categories he uses, his values—all of these are thoroughly Jewish even as Matthew evidences strong conflict with leaders and perspectives within the Jewish community. Matthew's community, he contends, was a "deviant" group within the more dominant context of emerging Pharisaic Judaism. Saldarini uses "deviant" in a technical not a moral sense: that is, a group which does not conform to mores or norms as defined by the majority or dominant group within a society. But being "deviant" does not automatically put one outside the group. "Within Judaism, Matthew's smaller group is viewed by the majority as deviant. Matthew's group has deviated from some of the culturally accepted ways of acting and thinking Jewishly, but it has not ceased to be Jewish in outlook, behavior, and identity. The author of Matthew hopes to convince the larger society to adopt its different behavior and outlook, so that it will become normative and no longer deviant" (p. 109). For Saldarini, therefore, Matthew (and his Gospel) is not "Jewish Christian" but "Christian Jewish."

But other important interpreters of Matthew are not convinced that Matthew and his community consider themselves still within the orbit of Judaism. Some, for example, believe that the gospel passages that severely critique the Jewish leaders are, in fact, vestiges of earlier stages in the development of Matthew's tradition. A representative of this viewpoint is Douglas Hare in his book *The Theme of Jewish Persecution of Christians in the Gospel According to St. Matthew*.[13] As the title of his study indicates, Hare's primary goal is to investigate the scope and nature of the persecution experienced by Christian missionaries, particularly in the post-70 period. Bitter texts such as Matthew 23:29-39 and 10:16-37 stem from the rejection of Christian missionaries by the synagogues of Pharisaic Judaism. This failure of the Christian mission to Israel had a deep influence on Matthew's sense of salvation history: now the offer of salvation was turned toward the Gentiles (28:16-20). Thus in its past history Matthew's community had experienced a painful and definitive rupture with Judaism.

In his important study of Matthew's theology entitled *Der Weg der Gerechtigkeit* ("The Way of Righteousness"), Georg Strecker had asserted the same view: Matthew's community had made a definitive break with Judaism.[14] Strecker assembled an imposing list of evidence: Matthew speaks of "their" scribes (7:29) and "their" synagogues (4:23; 9:35; 10:17; 12:9; 13:54). In comparison to parallel passages in Mark and Luke, Matthew intensifies polemical references to the Pharisees (see 15:12-14; 23:25-26). The title "rabbi," which is often used in Mark to refer respectfully to Jesus (Mk 9:5; 11:21; 14:45), is found in Matthew only on the lips of Judas (26:25, 49). And the disciples are warned not to take on the title "rabbi" (23:7-8). These are clear signals of alienation from Pharisaic Judaism. At the same time Matthew shows an openness to the Gentiles (28:19; 21:43, etc.), a sharp contrast with his hostility to the leaders of Judaism.

Similar views are held by David Garland and Sjef Van Tilborg in their independent studies of Matthew's strong attacks on the Jewish leaders.[15] In their reconstructions of the circumstances of Matthew's community, the strife between Matthew's community and the Jewish leaders is past history, now used symbolically in the gospel to characterize unfaithful responses to the teaching of Jesus.

In his major new commentary on Matthew's gospel, Ulrich Luz adds another emphatic point to this discussion.[16] He also believes that Matthew's community "no longer belongs to the Jewish synagogue system. The fissure between community and synagogue is final" (p. 88). Matthew is not attempting to interact with the Jewish community but wants to put Israel's rejection of Jesus in a theological perspective. "Thus," Luz says, "it has become clear that the Gospel of Matthew is not a Christian answer to 'Jamnia.' Rather it is a Christian answer to Israel's no to Jesus or the attempt to cope with this no in a fundamental definition of a position."

Therefore, for these Matthean interpreters the community that produced the gospel had already severed its ties with Pharisaic Judaism, a wrenching break that left the imprint of its wounds on Matthew's theological perspective.

Jew or Gentile?

Given the fact that Matthew's gospel seems to struggle with so many explicitly Jewish issues, most commentators assume that the evangelist himself was a Jewish Christian. Hummel, for example, considers Matthew to be a converted scribe of the Pharisee party.[17] Hare suggests that the bitter tones in Matthew's references to Judaism are due to the pain of separation from his own people.[18]

But still some scholars maintain that even though Matthew's community had Jewish-Christian roots, the evangelist himself was a Gentile. An early defender of this position was the Swedish author Poul Nepper-Christensen in his book, *Das Matthäusevangelium. Ein judenchristliches Evangelium?*[19] A more recent proponent is John Meier in his study of Matthew's theology entitled *The Vision of Matthew: Christ, Church and Morality in the First Gospel.*[20] He notes that Matthew's antagonism to Pharisaic Judaism is hard to reconcile with Jewish authorship. Meier points to such texts as the denunciation of the Jewish leaders in chapters 15 and 23 and 27:25 where the "whole people" accept responsibility for the innocent blood of Jesus. Meier also contends that on occasion Matthew makes errors about things Jewish. For example, the evangelist seems to be confused about the differences between the Sadducees and the Pharisees, as can be seen in 16:6 and 12, where Matthew refers to the "leaven of the Pharisees and Sadducees" (in contrast to Mark 8:15 which states the "leaven of the Pharisees and the leaven of Herod"). The evangelist explicitly interprets "leaven" as a metaphor for their "teaching" (Mt 16:12). The problem is that these two groups did not share a uniform "teaching" or "doctrine," as Matthew's phrase implies. On such key issues as the interpretation of law and the doctrine of resurrection the

Sadducees and Pharisees were at loggerheads. Meier believes further ambiguity about the Sadducees can be detected in Matthew 22:23 where instead of the historically precise identification of the Sadducees as those "who say there is no resurrection" (as in Mark 12:18 and Luke 20:27) Matthew's text reads, "...Sadducees, saying there is no resurrection," as if this were the conviction of some particular Sadducees and not the tenet of the entire party.

Meier sees another Matthean "error" in the evangelist's excessively literal reading of Zechariah 9:9 in the account of Jesus' triumphant entry into Jerusalem. In Matthew's rendition of the scene (again in contrast to the parallel in Mark 11:1-10), the disciples are instructed to prepare "an ass...and a colt" and Jesus sits on both (cf. Mt 21:7)! Commentators have traditionally explained this as Matthew's attempt to see a literal fulfillment of Zechariah 9:9 in this event of Jesus' life. Meier, however, thinks this also shows that Matthew misunderstands the Hebrew parallelism of Zechariah 9:9 where the reference to a donkey and a colt is not to two animals, but to one. Meier contends that only someone unfamiliar with Hebrew poetic forms, and, therefore, not a Jew, would be this literal on such an insignificant detail. Therefore, Matthew was not a Jew who became a Christian but a Gentile Christian who became well versed in the Hebrew scriptures and things Jewish.

The debate on this issue is not closed, but it should be noted that a majority of scholars continue to maintain that the evangelist was a Jewish Christian. The gospel's occasional bitter critique of the Jewish leaders can be explained by the rupture between the church and the synagogue. And Matthew's alleged "errors" are extremely subtle and capable of explanation. As we shall note below, many scholars locate Matthew's church in Hellenistic or diaspora Judaism, somewhere in the Roman empire outside of Palestine. Therefore Matthew was somewhat removed from the culture and circumstances of the Judaism Jesus knew.

Where? When? and Who?

Scholarship continues its sleuth work on these traditional questions about the origin of the gospel. Classical assumptions about Matthew were that it was the first gospel written, was authored by the apostle Matthew, and was, therefore, written somewhere in Palestine. All of these assumptions have been challenged.

The conclusions of Jack Dean Kingsbury in his introductory volume on the gospel offer a good synthesis of representative critical scholarship.[21] Kingsbury suggested that Matthew's community may have been located in Antioch of Syria, where there was a mixed population of Jews and Gentiles. The probable date of the gospel is around A.D. 85 or 90, some twenty years after the destruction of Jerusalem (A.D. 70), which Matthew alludes to in 22:7, and after the writing of Mark's gospel which Matthew seems to have used as a source.[22]

Kingsbury bases these conclusions on the profile that begins to emerge from a close examination of the gospel. First of all the language spoken by Matthew's community was Greek. The Greek style of Matthew is of good quality, not the kind of "translation Greek" that a native Hebrew or Aramaic speaker would be likely to use. At the same time, the Jewish tone of Matthew's gospel suggests that a majority of his community was Greek-speaking Jews.

Kingsbury also believes that Matthew's church was "urban and prosperous." Matthew refers to cities some twenty-six times and to villages only four times (by contrast, Mark refers to cities eight times and to villages seven times). Instead of simply the "poor" (Lk 6:20) Matthew's Jesus blesses the "poor in spirit" (5:3). And Matthew frequently escalates the value and amounts of money referred to in the gospel. For example in Mark 6:8 Jesus commands the disciples to take "no copper coins" with them on their journeys; in Matthew's version (10:9) that is inflated to no "gold, nor silver, nor copper coin." Luke's parable of the minas (19:11-27) escalates in Matthew to the parable of the talents (25:14-30), an amount fifty times more valuable than a mina. In Mark (15:43) and Luke (23:50-51), Joseph of Arimathea is identified as a member of the sanhedrin, but Matthew describes Joseph as "a rich man...who was also a disciple of Jesus" (27:57). In fact throughout his gospel Matthew refers to "gold" and "silver" more times than Mark and Luke combined.

Kingsbury allies himself with the opinion discussed above which places Matthew's community outside of the synagogue. Matthew's Jewish Christians had made a break with their counterparts in Pharisaic Judaism and now a sizable number of Gentiles were members of the community as well. As Kingsbury puts it: "[The Matthean community is] a church with members of Jewish and Gentile background which stands outside the orbit of official Judaism but lives in close proximity to both Jews and Gentiles, [and] encounters from without persecution on the part of both Jew and Gentile" (p. 103).

Antioch of Syria, a large urban center with a mixed population of Jews and Gentiles, seems to fit this description, as suggested in the work of R. Brown and J. Meier, *Antioch and Rome*.[23] As Meier notes in his section of this collaborative work, "As a whole...Matthew's gospel reflects a meeting place and melting pot of Jewish and Gentile influences. Antioch is a perfect location for this encounter and clash" (p. 23). R. Stark has offered a vivid description of the difficult social circumstances in a first century city such as Antioch and suggests that the mission of the Matthean community with its emphasis on healing and compassion would be warmly welcomed.[24]

But not all scholars agree that Antioch is the only possible place. A few have suggested Alexandria, mainly because of Matthew's tradition about the flight into Egypt in 2:13-15, or Phoenicia.[25] The American scholar Benedict Viviano put forward Caesarea Maritima, a lavish port city developed by Herod the Great, as a place which fulfills all the conditions reflected in the gospel (urban, prosperous, mixed population).[26] In addition, Caesarea has the advantage of being in Palestine, thus locating Matthew's community closer to the center of the Pharisaic reform. Viviano also argues that Caesarea became one of the earliest and most vigorous centers of Christian learning, a possible explanation for the literary and theological sophistication of Matthew. J. Andrew Overman suggests a Galilean location, perhaps the Greco-Roman city of Sepphoris, not far from Nazareth. A Palestinian location such as this would put Matthew's community in direct confrontation with Pharisaic Judaism (as Overman contends is the case), in a Galilean setting which the gospel seems to favor over Jerusalem, and in a large urban center.[27]

Although the location of Matthew's church will continue to be debated, a stronger consensus about authorship has emerged to the extent that few scholars are willing to identify the evangelist with the apostle Matthew. Kingsbury's viewpoint is representative: The evangelist was most probably not the apostle because: (1) Matthew depends on Mark as his main source and, therefore, does not seem to be an eyewitness; (2) the theological concerns and perspectives of Matthew are those of a "second generation" Christian; and (3) if the gospel is written around A.D. 85-90, the apostle Matthew was probably already dead.

However, the ancient church tradition that assigned the gospel to the apostle Matthew is not dismissed out of hand by Kingsbury and other recent scholars such as W.D. Davies.[28] The second century church writer Papias asserted that "Matthew wrote the oracles in the Hebrew language and everyone interpreted them as he was able." As we will discuss below, this led to a hypothesis about an original Aramaic edition of the gospel.[29] But Papias' information may not be accurate. In the gospel itself is the intriguing text where Mark's account of the call of Levi (2:14) is changed in Matthew to the call of the tax collector "Matthew" (cf. 9:9). Matthew makes a corresponding change in his list of apostles in 10:3. Other evidence may rule out Matthew as the final author of the gospel, but perhaps the apostle was associated in some way with the origin of Matthew's community. About this there can only be speculation.

Conclusion

Was Matthew's community still part of Judaism or not? The differences in views between an author like Saldarini on the one hand and Luz on the other seem irreconcilable on this point. However, closer examination indicates that there is some important middle ground. First of all, almost all of these hypotheses about the setting of Matthew's community point to a church in transition. The evangelist wrote for a group of Christians who were undergoing a transformation from a predominantly Jewish Christian church to an increasingly Gentile church, from a church whose roots and cultural origin were Palestinian to a church plunged into the midst of the Roman empire. The destruction of Jerusalem by the Romans signaled the end of the form of Judaism known to Jesus and to the earliest apostolic church. Both Judaism and Jewish Christianity had to strike a new course. This search for identity and for continuity within discontinuity seems to have been one of the primary purposes of Matthew's gospel.[30]

And terms such as "separation" and "belonging" do not have a uniform meaning in the studies we have considered. Virtually all recent studies on Matthew's gospel would agree that this evangelist and his community have strong roots in Judaism and that Matthew's gospel was concerned with such Jewish issues as fidelity to the law and the destiny of God's people. And all would agree that the community's faith in Jesus as the messiah, as God's authoritative teacher and redeemer, is the fundamental reason for the tension with the rest of the Jewish community and the basis upon which Matthew's community would ultimately take on a different self-identity. While staunchly defending his view that Matthew is within the orbit of Judaism, Saldarini admits that Matthew's community felt "separated" from the dominant Jewish group while still struggling to influence it.[31] And even though Matthew's categories and assumptions are thoroughly Jewish, he will also concede that the status and authority given to Jesus by Matthew's community is without precedent or peer in any other Jewish sect (p. 193). And both Overman and Saldarini, for example, will also concede that if Matthew's "Christian Jews" are still within the orbit of Judaism at the time the gospel is written, the break with Judaism and immersion within a Christian identity are right over the horizon. As Saldarini writes, "Thus Matthew's gospel entered the mainstream of the non-Jewish, second-century Christian church soon after it was written, but not in the lifetime or intention of the author" (p. 113).

Luz is correct, therefore, in insisting on the importance of Christology for Matthew. While interacting with the wider community of Judaism may have been part of Matthew's agenda, the primary purpose of his gospel is to encourage his readers to understand reality, past, present and future, in the light of Jesus.

2
The Sources and Structure of the Gospel

Introduction

This chapter considers two issues which probe beneath the surface of Matthew's gospel: (1) On what sources did Matthew draw for the contents of his gospel? (2) What structure or plot did he use to give shape to his story?

Both of these questions continue to be a concern of biblical scholarship because attempting to answer those questions helps the reader of the gospel determine the purpose and meaning of Matthew's text. We shall sample some of the scholarly work done in each area.

I. The Sources for Matthew's Gospel

At least from the time of Augustine of Hippo (fifth century A.D.) it was assumed that the canonical order of the gospels—Matthew, Mark, Luke, John—was in fact their historical order. Matthew was considered to be the first gospel written, its author an apostle and eyewitness to events of the gospel.

But modern biblical scholarship has challenged these assumptions. In the latter part of the nineteenth century, scholars developed a hypothesis about the interrelationship of the gospels which came to be known as the "two-source" theory.[1] Noting the striking similarities between Mark on the one hand and Matthew and Luke on the other, and the fact that Matthew and Luke had material in common but not present in Mark, scholars became convinced that Mark, not Matthew, was the first to be written. Matthew and Luke, independently of each other, used Mark as a primary source for their own versions of the gospel. Matthew, for example, takes over more than 600 of Mark's 661 verses. In addition, Matthew and Luke (again independently of each other) had access to another "source" which was dubbed "Q" (after the German word *Quelle* or "source"). This material shared by Matthew and Luke was primarily sayings material (as, for example, much of the material in Matthew's sermon on the mount [chaps. 5–7] and Luke's sermon on the plain [Lk 6:17-49]), although it also contained parables (see the parable of the lost sheep in Mt 18:12-13 and Lk 15:3-7) and healing stories (compare the accounts of the healing of the centurion's servant in Mt 8:5-13 and Lk 7:1-10). Authors speculated that the so-called "Q" document may have been a collection of Jesus' sayings that circulated among some of the early Christian communities. Opinion is divided on whether this collection was written or passed on orally. At any rate, Q provided Matthew and Luke with important additional material for the revision of Mark's gospel.

This, in very schematic form, is what is meant by the "two-source" theory: in composing his gospel, Matthew had access to two major sources, the gospel of Mark and Q. Not all of the material in Matthew's narrative is accounted for by these two sources. There are a significant number of passages in the gospel unique to Matthew such as the infancy narratives of chapters 1–2, the parable of the sheep and the goats in 25:31-46, the account of the guards at the tomb in 27:62-66 and 28:11-15, and many more examples. Scholars debate whether these special stories come from some special source (sometimes designated as "M" for Matthew) or whether in some instances the evangelist drew the stories from the traditions of his church or even freely composed them himself.

The great majority of Matthean interpreters today accept the two-source theory as a working hypothesis, even though many of them admit that it does not explain all of the complex data of the gospel's origin. By contrasting Matthew's rendition of a passage with his presumed source Mark or Q, the interpreter can detect what specific perspective the evangelist has introduced by means of his alterations, expansions or abbreviations. Thus the two-source theory has been the launching pad for many of the conclusions of redaction criticism.

For example, in a study defending the two-source theory, Gunther Bornkamm, one of the pioneer redaction critics, had used the so-called community discourse of chapter 18 as a test case.[2] He concluded that the discourse is a "mosaic" of Matthew's sources: from Mark (compare Mt 18:1-5 and Mk 9:33-37; Mt 18:6-9 and Mk 9:42-48), from Q (the parable in Mt 18:12-13, compare Lk 15:3-7, and the sayings in 18:21-22, compare Lk 17:4), and from Matthew's own special traditions (Mt 18:15-17 and the concluding section on forgiveness, 18:23-35). Bornkamm is convinced that awareness of how Matthew combines and adapts the various sources brings the interpreter closer to Matthew's meaning in the passage. In my own work on Matthew's passion narrative I found the same striking confirmation of Matthew's dependence on Mark in a section of the gospel where the two accounts are extremely similar.[3]

Challenges to the Two-Source Hypothesis

But in this issue, like most others, biblical scholarship does not walk in lockstep. There have been a number of challenges to the two-source theory.

Abbot B.C. Butler in his 1951 work *The Originality of St. Matthew* attacked the two-source theory head-on.[4] He maintained that Matthew's gospel was the first and that it was the major source for Mark. Some Catholic authors such as Vosté had attempted to maintain the tradition of Matthew's priority by asserting that the original version (now lost) had been in Aramaic, not Greek. Mark's Greek version depended on this Aramaic Matthew, while the Greek edition of Matthew used both Aramaic Matthew and Mark. This hypothesis wanted to reconcile both camps—Matthean priority and a semblance of the two-source theory (with its Markan priority).

But Abbot Butler was much bolder. His hypothesis was that Mark depended directly on the Greek gospel of Matthew. He also affirmed the tradition of Papias that connected the gospel of Mark with Peter. The apostle used Matthew's text as his *aide-memoire*, selecting passages "which his own memory could confirm and enlarge upon," and omitting incidents "that occurred before he met our Lord" (p. 168). In this way

Butler hoped to circumvent a major objection to the theory of Matthean priority, that is, why Mark would eliminate from his narrative such major chunks of the gospel of Matthew as the infancy narrative and the sermon on the mount.

Butler's hypothesis did not receive universal or enthusiastic acceptance, but it was not the last dissent to the two-source theory. An American scholar William R. Farmer has mounted a systematic challenge to the prevailing consensus in his revival of the Griesbach hypothesis which claimed that Matthew wrote first and that Luke expanded on Matthew, while Mark, in turn, used both Matthew and Luke in writing his gospel.[5] A challenge in another direction came from Michael D. Goulder in his work *Midrash and Lection in Matthew*.[6] He affirmed Matthew's literary dependence on Mark but denied that there was any Q source at all. Matthew, in Goulder's viewpoint, was extraordinarily creative; he did not depend on any special source other than Mark but freely composed those passages not found in Mark in order to serve the liturgical and catechetical needs of his church. Matthew, Goulder suggested, operated as a Christian scribe, expounding his interpretation of the gospel as the Jewish scribes did of the Torah.

The challenges come full circle with a theory such as that proposed in the Anchor Bible commentary on Matthew by W.F. Albright and C.S. Mann.[7] They question whether there is any direct literary relationship among the synoptic gospels at all and hold that a more probable explanation for the similarities among the three is the existence of a very early Aramaic or Hebrew gospel which was the common source for all three of the evangelists.

Despite these and many other proposed solutions to the synoptic problem, it remains true that the two-source theory is the dominant hypothesis among interpreters of Matthew's gospel. Several recent commentaries on Matthew explicitly work from the two-source hypothesis as the best practical solution to the interrelationship of the gospels.[8] The challenges, while failing to dissuade most exegetes from the two-source theory, do have some healthy effects. For one, they caution exegetes against making the two-source hypothesis an overly rigid dogma. It is only a hypothesis, even though the most plausible one, and it does not explain everything about Matthew's use of sources with equal clarity (cf., for example, the question of the "minor agreements"—those cases where Matthew and Luke have identical wording in passages over against both Mark and Q).[9]

Secondly, the hypothetical nature of all theories about Matthew's use of sources has cautioned exegetes against relying too exclusively on such theories for an interpretation of Matthew's text. The ultimate goal of redaction criticism is not to catalogue Matthew's alterations of his source material but to appreciate the overall meaning of the text as we now have it. This point was made by William Thompson in his book *Matthew's Advice to a Divided Community: Mt. 17, 22–18, 35.*[10] There are two dimensions to the redaction critic's work: (1) the "horizontal," in which the text of Matthew is compared with the parallel accounts of Mark and Luke in order to determine how Matthew has adapted his source material; (2) and the "vertical," that is, analyzing the style, structure and flow of an individual passage within the ongoing context of Matthew's gospel. This vertical dimension is the more essential one, Thompson claims, because "...the evangelist's interpretation of tradition will ultimately emerge only from a study of individual pericopes in their own composition and in relation to their surrounding context and the gospel as a whole" (p. 9).

This attention to the literary features of the gospel text allies redaction criticism with literary criticism, a growing force in modern biblical studies. The evangelists are not mere collectors of tradition but genuine authors, shaping their narratives from their own theological perspective and with their individual literary skill. The biblical scholar, therefore, should be sensitive to the literary dynamics of the biblical text, concerned not simply with the historical circumstances that stand behind this text, nor with what may have been the "intention" of the author, but with the shape and meaning of the text as it now stands before the reader.

II. The Structure of Matthew's Gospel

If Matthew is a genuine author, then we should expect his gospel story to have all the elements of a story, including that of a "plot" or structure. What passages or features of Matthew's narrative tip us off to the way the evangelist intended to move his reader through the story? Wrestling with this question, too, can help us discover the meaning of Matthew's gospel with more depth and precision. As in the question of sources no single solution has been found, but many of the proposed structures throw light on different facets of the gospel.

In a work entitled *The Structure of Matthew's Gospel*, David Bauer catalogues three major approaches taken by biblical scholarship on this issue.[11] (1) "geographical–chronological" structures that believe the gospel is organized according to the broad geographical layout of Jesus' story (e.g., Galilee/Jerusalem) and the sequence of events within Jesus' life (birth, baptism, public ministry, journey to Jerusalem, passion and resurrection); (2) "topical" structures which depend on patterns according to which the evangelist has ordered certain material in the gospels (e.g., the discourses or the unfolding of certain basic themes); (3) "conceptual" structures that are based on what scholars detect are underlying themes according to which the evangelist has established the order of materials in the gospel (e.g., salvation history).

Under what Bauer calls "topical" structures three approaches have been especially significant in studies of Matthew's narrative.

1. The Discourse Format

One of the most influential answers to the question of Matthew's structure was provided by an American scholar, Benjamin Bacon.[12] His so-called Pentateuchal theory is not widely accepted today, but Bacon highlighted certain aspects of Matthew's narrative that are featured in almost every attempt to solve the riddle of its structure.

Bacon noted the presence of a more or less fixed statement that occurred five times in Matthew's gospel (7:28; 11:1; 13:53; 19:1; 26:1). Each of these statements begins in similar fashion (for example, "And when Jesus finished these sayings..."—Mt 7:28) and each marks the boundary between a discourse section and a narrative section of the gospel. This phenomenon led Bacon to propose that the structure of Matthew's gospel was modeled after that of the five great books of the Pentateuch. Each of Matthew's "books" included both narrative and discourse (a pattern which Bacon felt could be traced in the five books of the Pentateuch as well), with the fivefold formula signaling the end of the discourse and, therefore, the end of each "book."

Matthew's intention, according to Bacon, was to present Jesus as a "new Moses," offering a new law to the church. In this way, Bacon surmised, Matthew, a converted rabbi, hoped to counteract lawlessness in his own church.

Bacon's thesis was clear and attractive, but under close scrutiny it did not hold up. The most important objection was that Bacon's five-book framework left out some crucial Matthean passages. Bacon had relegated the infancy narratives of chapters 1 and 2 and the passion and resurrection accounts of chapters 26–28 to "prologue" and "epilogue" respectively, because they did not fit into his five-book format. But these major parts of the gospel hardly stand on the periphery of Matthew's story about Jesus! Bacon's proposal also overlooks other discourses present in Matthew which are not marked off by the five formulae, such as the speeches in 11:7-30 and 23:1-39. Secondly, it is not clear that the formula which Bacon believed concluded the books of Matthew is really a concluding formula at all. On face value those five verses seem more like transitional statements that move the reader along to the next section after a discourse is finished. And, finally, Bacon's theory suggested that Matthew wanted to depict Jesus as the "new Moses." While this is a motif in Matthew's gospel, it may not have the overall importance that Bacon assigned to it.[13]

While Bacon's "Pentateuchal" structure is not accepted today, other scholars have tried variations on this theme. Hubert Frankemölle in a major study of Matthew's theology entitled *Jahwebund und Kirche Christi* ("Covenant of Yahweh and Church of Christ") found Old Testament inspiration for Matthew's discourses not in the fivefold structure of the Pentateuch but in the book of Deuteronomy.[14] Frankemölle noted the similarities between the transition formula, especially that of 26:1, and Deuteronomy 31:1, 24 and 32:44-45. Like Matthew's gospel, Deuteronomy is a narrative interspersed with speeches; in fact the final formula is meant to bind together speech and narrative sections. And Moses' discourses, like those of Jesus in Matthew, end with warnings of judgment. Both Deuteronomy and Matthew emphasize the need to do good deeds. Frankemölle also sees a parallel in that Deuteronomy presents Moses as giving a series of farewell discourses to Israel as it stands on the brink of a new future; Matthew's Jesus seems to do the same thing for the church. Thus Frankemölle uses the discourses to retrieve the Mosaic motif of Bacon's theory but, ultimately, on completely different grounds.

Dale Allison also uses Bacon's theory as a starting point in developing his own very different analysis.[15] Allison believes that the alternation of narrative and discourse is the key to Matthew's structure. This alternation continues throughout the gospel: chaps. 1–4 (N); 5–7 (D), 8–9 (N), 10 (D), 11–12 (N), 13 (D), 14–17 (N), 18 (D), 19–23 (N), 24–25 (D), 27–28 (N). Within each narrative and discourse section, Allison contends, one can find a fairly consistent train of thought, and as the various segments accumulate throughout the gospel, the plot of Matthew emerges. Stated in succinct terms, the structure and plot of Matthew would be the following:

1–4	N	Introduction of the main character Jesus
5–7	D	Jesus' demands upon Israel
8–9	N	Jesus' deeds within and for Israel
10	D	Extension of ministry through words and deeds of others
11–12	N	Israel's negative response
13	D	Explanation of Israel's negative response
14–17	N	Establishment of the new people of God, the church
18	D	Instruction to the church
19–23	N	Commencement of the passion, the beginning of the end
24–25	D	The future: judgment and salvation
26–28	N	Conclusion: the passion and resurrection

Allison believes that this structure highlights Matthew's focus on Jesus. The gospel is a "biography" of Jesus, calling the community to imitate his virtue and thus find the way of salvation.

2. Chiastic Patterns

Another important "topical" approach to the structure of Matthew is by detecting formal patterns in the way the evangelist arranges material. Everyone recognizes that Matthew brings more "order" to the gospel material than the other evangelists. His grouping of Jesus' sayings and parables into discourses, the collection of miracles in chapters 8 and 9, and judgment motifs in chapters 23–25 are evidence of this. Some scholars see Matthew's penchant for organization as a highly developed art leading to an intricate symmetrical pattern for the gospel as a whole.

Peter F. Ellis, in his popular study *Matthew: His Mind and His*

Message, dubbed the evangelist "meticulous Matthew" and believed that the evangelist shaped his gospel according to an intricate and comprehensive "chiastic" pattern.[16] Ellis agrees with Bacon and others that the sequence of narrative and discourse is important in Matthew's framework but the evangelist's overall plan is much more elaborate than Bacon had supposed.

First of all Ellis finds a symmetry running throughout the gospel. Like a literary mobile Matthew's discourses "hang" from a center point, the parable discourse of chapter 13. In this suspension, discourses in the two halves of the gospel parallel each other: the sermon on the mount of chapters 5–7 paralleling the judgment discourse of chapters 23–25; the mission discourse (chapter 10), in which the disciples are sent out, balanced by the community discourse (chapter 18), in which the "little ones" are received.

Ellis finds similar parallels in the narrative sections. For example the opening scenes of the gospel (chapters 1–4) correspond with the passion and resurrection story (chapters 26–27) and so on. The "chiastic" form can be seen in the following diagram:

Sermon		(f) ch 13 (f´)
Narratives	ch 11–12 (e)	(e´) ch 14–17
Sermons	ch10 (d)	(d´) ch 18
Narratives	ch 8–9(c)	(c´) ch 19–22
Sermons	ch 5–7(b)	(b´) ch 23–25
Narratives	ch 1–4(a)	(a´) ch 26–28[17]

Even this pattern does not exhaust Matthew's intricate planning in Ellis' view. He finds that the length of the discourses fits a pattern, too: the sermon on the mount roughly the same length as the discourse of chapters 23–25, and chapter 10 about the same length as chapter 18 and so on. Even the content of the discourses has a thematic relationship within the pattern, Ellis claims. For example, chapter 10 on the mission of the apostles parallels chapter 18's attention to the authority of the apostles within the community. In the first half of the gospel (up to the mid-point of chapter 13) Jesus speaks to all the Jews; after 13:35 Jesus turns his attention to the disciples. And, finally, Matthew's use of numbers is significant. Ellis' proposed framework counts five great discourses and two minor ones (3:8-12; 28:18-20), adding up to seven, a highly symbolic number favored by Matthew.

Ellis' proposed structure has to be commended for its ingenuity but a close look at this framework raises some questions. For example, Ellis considers chapters 11–12 as a "narrative," when in fact it has a lot of discourse material (cf. 11:7-30), much more, in fact, than what Ellis calls the "minor discourse" of 3:8-12 which is a discourse of John the Baptist, not Jesus. Several of the thematic relationships between sets of narratives or discourses seem quite tenuous, such as that between the miracle chapters of 8–9 and the variety of materials in chapters 19–22, or between the mission discourse of chapter 10 and the community discourse of chapter 18. The parallels Ellis suggest are so subtle that one wonders if the evangelist intended to build his gospel story in such a way or, if intended, readers would ever detect it.

In a recent study of Matthew's passion and resurrection account, John Paul Heil has proposed a variation on the sort of chiastic pattern detected by Ellis.[18] Using the method of "reader response" criticism that attends to the interaction between the text and the reader, Heil notes how Matthew anticipates later events in the gospel story. Thus the announcement in the infancy narrative that Jesus is the Christ anticipates his messianic work of healing and teaching that will take place in the body of the gospel. Similarly, the opposition of the Jewish leaders during the ministry of Jesus anticipates the passion story. Such patterns lead Heil to uncover an elaborate formal schema in chapters 26–28 of Matthew's gospel, in which the evangelist divides the material into three major sections (26:1-56; 26:57–27:54; 27:55–28:20), each of which is composed of three sets of alternating and contrasting scenes. For example, 26:1-56 is divided into 26:1-16; 26:17-29 and 26:30-56. The first segment, 26:1-16, entitled "Jesus prepares for and accepts his death," has three alternating scenes— the Jewish leaders plot Jesus' death (26:1-5), the death of Jesus is anticipated at a meal (26:6-13) and a disciple plans to betray Jesus (26:14-16). Heil extends this type of schema through the passion narrative and, by implication, throughout Matthew's gospel. While his method does point to many of the contrasts and links in Matthew's story, at times the structure he sees in Matthew seems forced and overly elaborate.[19]

There is little doubt that Matthew used some formal patterns to order the material in his gospel. Luz, for example, points to the evangelist's predilection for strings of three (e.g., there are three segments in the following sections of the gospel: 1:18–2:23; 5:21–7:11; 8:1-17; 9:1b-17 and so on) and the probability that he has arranged the discourses in a certain pattern according to length: the first, the sermon on the mount (chaps. 5–7), and the fifth, the apocalyptic discourse (chaps. 24–25), are the longest; the second, the mission discourse (ch. 10), and the fourth, the community discourse (ch. 18), are the shortest, and the middle discourse, the parable discourse (ch. 13), is medium-sized.[20] Yet it is unlikely that the entire structure of the gospel can be ordered according to any single formal pattern.

3. "From that time…"

Other scholars under the category of what Bauer considers "topical" structures find the key to Matthew's overall structure or plot not in the narrative and discourse sequence or in formal patterns but in another set of signals. Twice in his gospel Matthew uses a similar statement, beginning with the phrase "From that time Jesus began…" (cf. 4:17 and 16:7). Some authors, such as Jack Dean Kingsbury, following the lead of Edgar Krentz and others, believe that this phrase marks the boundaries of the major divisions of the gospel.[21] The words "from that time" show that by means of this formula the evangelist wanted to indicate "the beginning of a new phase in the life of Jesus" (p. 8). Each of the formula signals the major theme of the section it introduces. The formula in 4:17 reads, "From that time Jesus began to preach, saying, 'Repent, for the kingdom of heaven is at hand,'" thereby introducing that major section of the gospel where Jesus' public proclamation is described. In 16:21 the formula reads, "From that time Jesus began to show his disciples that he must go to Jerusalem and suffer many things from the elders and chief priests and scribes, and be killed, and on the third day be raised," thus introducing the major part of the gospel dealing with the suffering, death and resurrection of Jesus the messiah.

To complete his outline Kingsbury has to contend with the section from chapter 1 up to 4:16. He believes that the opening verse of the gospel—"the book of the origin of Jesus Christ, son of David, the son of Abraham" (1:1)—functions analogously to the formulae in 4:17 and 16:21, that is, it serves as introduction to the whole section of 1:2–4:16

where the "origin" of Jesus is described in order that the reader can have proper understanding of his person. Therefore, Kingsbury's outline of Matthew is complete:

I. 1:1–4:16 The Person of Jesus the Messiah
II. 4:17–16:20 The Proclamation of Jesus Messiah
III. 16:21–28:20 The Suffering, Death and Resurrection of Jesus Messiah

Kingsbury first proposed this outline in a series of redactional studies on Matthew's gospel but in recent years he has turned to literary critical methods in his study of the gospel. In a work entitled *Matthew as Story* he analyzed in detail the structure of Matthew.[22] Employing the terminology of the literary critic Seymour Chatman, Kingsbury notes that as a narrative Matthew's gospel is comprised of two major parts: the "story" and its "discourse." The "story" of Matthew's gospel is, in effect, the life of Jesus from birth to resurrection. The "discourse" is composed of all the means the evangelist uses to tell this story. In turn, three basic elements characterize Matthew's discourse: the string of events or the "plot" (which, in Matthew's case, Kingsbury believes is strongly driven by conflict); the "characters" (e.g., Jesus, the disciples, the religious leaders, the crowds and other minor characters) and the "settings" (defined as the "place or time or social circumstances in which a character acts"). All of these combine and interact to give Matthew's gospel its particular flavor and point of view.

In applying this literary critical analysis to Matthew, Kingsbury arrives at the same basic structure described above that he had detected using redactional critical methods.[23] Of course, along the way he provides insight into many features of Matthew's gospel. However, the reader will have to decide whether arriving at the identical conclusion by employing two very different methods confirms the solidity of literary critical methods or questions their usefulness.

Whether this threefold division solves the question of Matthew's masterplan is, in any case, debatable.[24] Certainly Kingsbury's broad division of the gospel does coincide with the major movements of Matthew's story, but did Matthew intend these specific time references as the linchpins of the whole structure and as signals for fundamental motifs that carry his story of Jesus forward?

A strong critique of Kingsbury's thesis has been mounted by Frans Neirynck in a detailed study entitled "*Apo Tote Erkzato* and the Structure of Matthew."[25] He first of all questions marking the beginning of Jesus' public ministry at 4:17. The actual beginning commences at 4:12 where Jesus hears of the Baptist's arrest and enters Galilee. Neirynck would prefer, therefore, to see the entire section 4:12-17 as the beginning of Jesus' ministry. The phrase *apo tote* ("from that time") is an important transition phrase, catching up the preceding reference to the end of the Baptist's ministry (and thus the preparatory events of the opening segment of the gospel) as well as the fulfillment text that signals Jesus' entry in the arena of Galilee (4:13-16); the phrase is also "prospective," signaling the events that are to come (summarized in the reference to Jesus' proclamation of the approaching kingdom of heaven).

Neirynck makes a similar point about 16:21. Designating this verse as a major turning point in the gospel breaks up the unity of the story about Peter that runs from 16:13 to 16:23 where Matthew narrates both the positive and negative aspects of his portrait of the apostle.[26] Neirynck agrees that 16:13-23 signals a major turning point in the story, and 16:21 with its first explicit passion prediction surely emphasizes this new phase. But the entire passage—not a single verse—should be taken into account. Neirynck observes that Matthew also uses the phrase *apo tote* in 26:16. Kingsbury and others defending the tripartite division do not consider this on a parallel with 4:17 and 16:21 since it does not contain the verb "begin" and refers directly to Judas', not Jesus' fate.[27] Yet, as Neirynck, points out, 26:16 comes at a crucial phase of the passion story, surely one of the major phases of Matthew's plot.[28] Here we can see the function of *apo tote* in Matthew: it catches up previous events (i.e., the lead into the passion story culminating in Judas' plot with the religious leaders) and points ahead to the unfolding events of arrest, trial and crucifixion.

Neirynck goes on to make some other important observations about Matthew's structure. In determining the overall plot of Matthew, interpreters should not overlook the evangelist's use of his source, Mark. Mt 4:12, for example, parallels what is clearly a transition point in Mark's story (1:14) where, after John's arrest, Jesus enters Galilee and announces his proclamation of the kingdom of God. And keeping an eye on Matthew's reaction to Mark (as well as Q), it is clear that 4:23–11:1

is a section of the gospel where the evangelist has exercised more editorial freedom than any other part of the gospel. These factors need to be taken into account in tracing the flow of Matthew's story.

Finally, Neirynck points to a key factor in reading Matthew. He notes that in fact the two verses that Kingsbury and others see as thematic headings for major sections of the gospel are not identical in function. Mt 4:17, as part of the entire passage 4:12-17, is the beginning of Jesus' public ministry. But this public ministry does not end with 16:20! In other words, 16:21 (again as an integral part of the entire transition passage 16:13-23) signals a new phase in the gospel with its prediction of Jesus' passion but the proclamation of the kingdom of God announced in 4:12-17 *continues* to the end of the gospel. Thus 4:17 has an overall thematic function that is not true of 16:21.[29]

Understanding Matthew's Structure

Neirynck's caution about using a single formula as a thematic marker in Matthew's structure and his reminder to take into account the evangelist's potential reaction to source material are important. Every "solution" to the question of Matthew's master plan (and there are many more than the ones illustrated here) has some flaws. This has led some scholars to wonder if the question is being posed in the correct way. What exactly do we mean by "structure"? Should this be thought of as a detailed and comprehensive outline that the evangelist consciously designed beforehand and then proceeded to write his gospel in rigid adherence to this blueprint? Such a scenario is not impossible, of course, but the failure of scholars to agree about this master plan might suggest that Matthew did not proceed in such a mechanistic fashion.

Or did Matthew have a single idea or motif in mind as he sat down to compose his story, such as modeling the gospel on the books of the Pentateuch or on Deuteronomy or choosing an alternating pattern of narrative and discourse or signaling turns in the plot by certain key phrases that in turn underscored themes or phases of Jesus' life? This approach, too, has its problems precisely because each motif or pattern suggested by scholars such as Bacon, Ellis, Frankemölle, Allison and Kingsbury has merit. Bauer, for example, points to seventeen different structural elements that can contribute to ultimately form the narrative structure of any literary work.[30]

This might mean that Matthew's "plan" was, in fact, much less systematic and much richer in variety than most scholars have thought. A storyteller does not work in the same way as a mathematician. The storyteller does not usually begin with a rigid comprehensive plan. Instead, as Kingsbury and others sensitive to the literary aspects of the gospels point out, the artistic mind of the narrator has some basic motifs he or she wants to express, some convictions about the characters who will people his or her story and the settings in which they will be placed, and some idea of the basic plot or story line, including its subplots.[31] Only as the author begins to assemble the cast of characters and to spin out the story does the full structure emerge from what to that point may have been hunches and semi-conscious intuitions rather than a clear blueprint.

This type of composition process may, in fact, be closer to the procedure that shaped the plot or structure of Matthew's gospel. After all, as recent exegesis has emphasized, the gospels are stories and the evangelists are storytellers. In Matthew's case, an important point sometimes neglected in literary analysis of Matthew's gospel is the likelihood that some of the lines of that story were already fixed for him by his source, the gospel of Mark. But Matthew had other sources and ideas he wanted to blend into his narrative. So his structure may best be described as a retelling of the story of Mark. He built his gospel around the basic story line provided by Mark (Jesus' public ministry in Galilee; a journey from Galilee to Jerusalem in the course of which Jesus predicts his passion and instructs his disciples; the final days in the Jerusalem temple and the climactic story of the passion and resurrection). But Matthew "retells" the story with his own touches, adding an infancy narrative, creating a series of discourses, extending the resurrection section to include appearances at the tomb and in Galilee, and so on. Even the materials he has taken over from Mark or Q are reshaped in Matthew's own style and perspective. The end result is a new telling of the traditional story of Jesus provided by Mark.

As Matthew moves the reader through his story there are several devices and motifs that carry the plot. In Bauer's terms, Matthew's narrative plan may be built from a combination of geographical, chronological, topical and conceptual elements. To these should be added reactions to the material provided by his major sources, Mark and

Q, and the interspersing of narrative and discourse. The structure of the gospel is more like the flowing lines of a symphony than the fixed girders supporting a building. Thus the great discourses with their concluding formulae and those key moments in the life of Jesus when he enters Galilee (4:12-17) or sets out for Jerusalem (16:21) and the rising crescendo of opposition which breaks out in chapters 11–13 are all important movements in Matthew's on-going narrative. All of them together function as seams or turns within the gospel's organic structure rather than as potential keys to a single fixed blueprint.

Keeping in mind the elements discussed above, we might hazard the following general sketch of Matthew's story line:

I. (1:1–4:11) The origin of Jesus is traced in his birth and infancy and in his encounter with John in the desert (the point where Matthew joins up with Mark's story).

II. (4:12–10:42) The entire scene of 4:12-17 (not just a single verse) is a key transition moment, bridging Jesus' contact with John the Baptist, announcing the start of his public ministry in Galilee and signaling the motif of the kingdom of heaven that will run throughout the gospel. The pace quickens as Matthew unfolds Jesus' Galilean ministry, ordered around teaching (chapters 5–7) and healing (chapters 8–9), a ministry designed to serve as a model for the apostles' own mission (chapter 10). It is noteworthy that in this section Matthew introduces significant material not found in Mark's gospel (e.g., the sermon on the mount; elements of the mission discourse) and imposes his own order (e.g., aligning the miracle stories of chapters 8 and 9). In the next section, particularly after the parable discourse of chapter 13, Matthew returns to the story line of Mark.

III. (11:1–16:12) A new phase of the story begins to emerge as Matthew shows varying responses to Jesus, both rejection by Jewish opponents (esp. chapters 11–12) and the glimmering faith of the disciples (esp. chapters 14–16).

IV. (16:13–20:34) Once again the entire Petrine story in 16:13-23 is a "bridge," with the blessing on Peter serving as a culmination of some of the discipleship themes apparent in the previous section and the orientation to the passion signaled in the passion prediction and the rebuke to Peter. The drama of the death and resurrection of Jesus looms as Matthew follows Mark's lead and presents Jesus and his disciples on the way to Jerusalem. Instructions to the disciples (e.g., chapter 18) as well as conflicts with the opponents (e.g., 19:3-9) continue throughout the journey.

V. (21:1–28:15) The holy city is the center of focus where Jesus has his final days of teaching in the temple area, and when all his teaching is done (26:1), the passion story begins, leading to death and resurrection;

VI. (28:16-20) Although it is only a single scene, this vivid finale (found only in Matthew) brings the gospel story full-term, back to Galilee where Jesus sends his disciples out into the world and promises his abiding presence. In so doing it is not simply the concluding part of the preceding section but recapitulates major themes of the gospel and directs the reader to the continuing life of the community that is to live out Jesus' commands and example.[32]

Such a "structure" is, of course, not as thematically consistent or as architecturally symmetrical as some of the others we have sampled. But it does, I think, take into account the major movements of Matthew's story. A "structure" that gives attention to the nature of Matthew's gospel as narrative, and therefore as a fluid, organic literary piece, one that takes into account his relationship to Mark's gospel, and that makes room for the particular theological motifs of Matthew, has the best chance of doing justice to the whole spectrum of Matthew's distinctive features.

3
Matthew's View of Salvation History

Introduction

One of the major reasons Matthew wrote his gospel was to give new perspective to a Christian community caught in the sweeping transition from a church mainly Jewish in character to one increasingly Gentile. This represents a strong consensus of contemporary scholarship, as we saw in Chapter 1 on "The Setting for Matthew's Gospel."

It is not surprising, therefore, that Matthew should give special attention to history. He begins his gospel story with a genealogy (1:2-18) that ties the life of Jesus back into the history of Israel, starting with Abraham, and moving through David and the time of the exile down to the advent of the messiah. Matthew constantly refers to the Old Testament, illustrating how Jesus "fulfilled" the promises given to Israel.[1] And Matthew's story ends with the risen Christ sending his apostles out on a mission that will take them not only to the ends of the earth, but to the end of time (28:19-20). Matthew's story, then, moves from the beginning to the end of sacred history.

At the same time there are other features of Matthew's gospel that are baffling when trying to knit together his overall perspective on history. In the midst of his public ministry, Jesus seems to restrict his mission and that of the disciples to Israel alone (see 10:5 and 15:24), but at the end of the gospel the apostles are sent to "all nations" (28:19). In the sermon on the mount, the Matthean Jesus declares that "not one letter, not one stroke of a letter" will pass away "until heaven and earth pass away" or "until all is fulfilled" (5:18). And when Jesus sends his disciples out on mission to the "lost sheep of the house of Israel" (10:6), he predicts that they will "not have gone through all the towns of Israel before the Son of Man comes" (10:23).

How one can piece all of this together into a coherent and meaningful perspective has been a significant topic for biblical research on Matthew. While no student of the gospel could deny that Matthew's narrative encompasses the whole of what we might call "sacred" or "salvation history," there is disagreement about how Matthew conceived of that history, and more recent approaches have called into the question the very notion of "salvation history."

Since the term "salvation history" is somewhat vague and subject to many interpretations, it is wise to define what is meant at the outset. John Meier, in his book *The Vision of Matthew*, offers a good working definition:

> By salvation history we mean a schematic understanding of God's dealings with men that emphasizes continuity—yet difference. Insofar as the theologian, reflecting on saving events, sees the one and same God acting faithfully and consistently within the flow of time, he perceives continuity, a basic horizontal line (though not always a straight one). Insofar as the theologian sees the different ways in which God acts at different times and the different ways in which man responds, he perceives the lines of demarcation which delimit the distinct periods of this history— the vertical lines of division, as it were. Difference within continuity, the various stages within the one divine economy: this is the basic insight on which any outline or pattern of salvation history is built.[2]

Salvation history, then, is a faith perspective; the believer looks back at the flow of historical events and detects a pattern which helps shape a religious consciousness of the present. Many of Matthew's fellow Christians may not have been able to see any continuity at all. They were cut off from or at least strained with their Jewish roots and facing an uncertain future, with streams of Gentiles, along with their strange customs and ignorance of Judaism, now flowing into the church. By reflecting on "continuity-within-discontinuity," Matthew intended to give new perspective and therefore new hope to his baffled church.[3] But exactly how did Matthew view this sacred or salvation history? What were its major turning points as it moved from Israel's past into the present of Matthew's church? To these questions contemporary Matthean scholars have given divergent answers.

A History in Three Stages

One of the earliest redaction critics to turn his attention exclusively to this question was Rolf Walker in his book *Die Heilsgeschichte im ersten Evangelium* ("Salvation History in the First Gospel").[4] Walker underscores Matthew's comprehensive schema that runs from Abraham (1:1) on one end to the consummation of the world on the other (28:20). Along the way, according to Walker, Matthew's gospel marks off key periods or stages in this sweep of sacred history.

The genealogy (1:1-18) shows that one major period, the premessianic age, runs from Abraham up to the birth of the messiah Jesus. The messianic age itself is cast into two major sub-periods. The first was the proclamation of the gospel of the kingdom to Israel. This is evident, Walker suggests, in Matthew's narrative where Jesus restricts his mission to the house of Israel (see 10:5; 15:24). That period continued for the duration of the church's mission to Israel up to A.D. 70 and the destruction of Jerusalem when the definitive failure of the Jewish mission became evident to Matthew's church. From that time on, a new and final period of history was in place: the mission to the Gentiles. This period, Walker argues, is signaled not only in the clear universal mission commission of 28:16-20 ("make disciples of all nations") but in Matthew's dual emphasis within the story of Jesus on Israel's rejection of Jesus and the favorable response of Gentiles (see, for example, the centurion of 8:5-15, and the Canaanite woman of 15:21-28).

In other words, for Walker, the drama of the gospel is a symbolic presentation of salvation history, a history that is worked out in three stages. The hostility between Jesus and the Jewish leaders is not reflective of a contemporary polemic between Matthew and Pharisaic Judaism but plays out the second stage of messianic salvation history in which the message of the kingdom is proclaimed to Israel. The leaders represent "Israel" which rejects the messiah and sets the stage for the third and final period of sacred history in which the message of the kingdom is offered to Gentiles. This is the period in which Matthew's church finds itself. Matthew's schematization of history, in Walker's view, helps ratify the Gentile mission and provides a way of understanding the tragic past.

Writing a bit earlier than Walker, George Strecker turned his attention to Matthew's historical perspective in an article entitled "Das Geschichtsverstandnis des Matthäus" ("The Concept of History in Matthew").[5] Strecker notes "historicizing tendencies" in Matthew, not only in the addition of the genealogy and infancy narrative to Mark's story line, but in other chronological references that reveal the evangelist's historical and chronological interest, as when Matthew adds the phrase "from that time" at key moments of the gospel story in 4:17; 16:21; 26:16.[6] Matthew also has geographical allusions that Strecker considers part of the "historicizing tendency." For example, Matthew alone designates Capernaum as Jesus' "own city" (9:1) and refers to Jesus "dwelling" in Capernaum (9:13). For Mark, by contrast, references to houses are not fixed geographically; they are merely settings in which Jesus' private instruction to his disciples is given (see Mk 2:1; 3:20; 7:17; 9:28, 33; 10:10).

Other aspects of the gospel reveal Matthew's interest in an historical perspective. Strecker appeals to the many Old Testament quotations which emphasize Jesus' fulfillment of the promises to Israel. In the infancy narrative these quotations are applied to the progressive stages of Jesus' own history: Bethlehem, Egypt, Nazareth, Capernaum. The same is true for the references to the mission: during the lifetime of Jesus it is restricted to Israel (10:5-6; 15:24); only after Jesus' death does it include Gentiles (28:19).

From this kind of evidence Strecker constructs what he believes is Matthew's view of salvation history. As in Walker's proposal Strecker maintains that in Matthew sacred time has a three-stage progression but its demarcations are slightly different than Walker's schema: (I) A time of preparation. This encompasses the history of Israel prior to Jesus. The patriarchs and prophets point forward to Jesus; the fate of the prophets (cf. 23:29-39) foreshadows Jesus' own. (II) The time of Jesus. In this period Jesus and his message of the kingdom are directed exclusively to the people of Israel. This period comes to an end with the life of Jesus, including the rejection of his call to repentance and the consequent loss of Israel's priority within salvation history (cf. 21:43). (III) The time of the church. This is a time of mission that is to last until the end of the world. This final age demands that the teaching of Jesus be carried out: it is to be a time of justice and obedience.

For Matthew, all of sacred history pivots around the life of Jesus. Matthew thereby provides continuity for his community, but at the same time, according to Strecker, the evangelist is able to press his major interest which is ethical: full response to the words and deeds of Jesus constitutes authentic righteousness in this climactic age which leads to the consummation of all history.

Both Walker and Strecker agree that the life of Jesus is central to Matthew's salvation history perspective. But the two authors part ways on which events flag key moments in the schema. For Walker, the failure of the mission to Israel and the opening to the Gentiles—events which take definite shape around the watershed date of A.D. 70—form the turning point. Matthew's "life of Jesus" is told in such a way that it reflects these later realities. Strecker, on the other hand, gives more emphasis to the past reality of Jesus' life up to his death and resurrection. His historical existence is the turning point between the past of Israel and the present of the church, and the ethical teaching and example of Jesus sets the pattern for authentic response in the last and decisive period of history.

Death–Resurrection as Turning Point

Another important example of a scholar who sees a tripartite division of history in Matthew is John Meier. First in an article entitled "Salvation History in Matthew: In Search of a Starting Point," and later in his doctoral dissertation *Law and History in Matthew's Gospel*, and in his book on Matthew's theology entitled *The Vision of Matthew* (a distillation of his thesis), Meier wrestles with this issue.[7] While accepting the general divisions of history into (a) the time of Israel, (b) the time of Jesus and (c) the time of the church, Meier does not attempt to sketch out the full spectrum of sacred history as Walker and Strecker had done; instead, he concentrates on the events of Jesus' life as presented by Matthew. He contends that it is not just the "life of Jesus" as such which represents the turning point of history for Matthew, but specifically the death and resurrection of Jesus. When Matthew describes the events that surround the moment of Jesus' death, he does so in a way that clearly signals his interpretation of these events (see 27:51-54): the temple veil is torn in two, and there is an earthquake, a shattering of the tombs and the triumphant raising of the holy ones of Israel from the dead. The tearing of the temple veil as a sign of God's judgment on the old dispensation is already present in Mark's gospel (Mk 15:38). But the earthquake and the resurrection of the dead are added by Matthew. These kinds of dramatic events are also found in apocalyptic writings of Judaism, such as the Book of Enoch, written roughly contemporary with Matthew. These were considered typical signs of the final age, the coming of the great day of the Lord when, as Meier notes, "Death is vanquished and must yield up its captives."[8] Matthew may have been inspired by the vision of Ezekiel 37:1-14 (especially vv. 7, 12-14) which presents new life coming to the dead bones of Israel. This passage apparently had special meaning for the Judaism of Matthew's era.[9]

Meier also notes that the finale of Matthew's death scene is the acclamation of Jesus by the centurion and his companions (27:54): "Indeed he was the Son of God." Therefore, Matthew presents the death (and ultimate victory) of Jesus as a decisive moment in sacred history: the old age symbolized by the temple is over, a new age of resurrection has begun, and the Gentiles are beginning to respond to Jesus.

The death scene in 27:51-54 is not the only place Matthew uses this kind of imagery. He follows through in his narration of the empty tomb story by enriching the account of his source Mark with more apocalyptic descriptions. As the women are coming to see the tomb, there is a "great earthquake," and a fearsome "angel of the Lord" with a radiant appearance causes the guards to fall into a tremor (28:2-4). These details, too, are similar to the way Jewish literature described the expected events of the final age (see, for example, Daniel 7:9; 10:5-6; 10:8, 16).

Meier believes that these passages help us interpret how Matthew viewed salvation history. The evangelist presents not just the life of Jesus in general as a turning point in salvation history but the very climax of his redemptive mission—death and resurrection—as the hinge on which that history turns. This helps fit into place other pieces of Matthew's narrative. The concluding passage of 28:16-20 where the risen Christ appears to his disciples on a Galilean mountain top and sends them out on a worldwide mission is a "proleptic parousia."[10] Matthew uses this scene to show Jesus as the Son of Man coming in triumph to his church, a foretaste of the final coming which will take place at the definitive consummation of history. But even now, Matthew's gospel insists, that triumphant parousia of the Lord is present in the church.

This view of history enables us in turn to understand how Matthew handled other issues of his gospel. Prior to the death and resurrection of Jesus, the mission is restricted to Israel (see 10:5-6; 15:24), but when the new age begins at the cross the mission can become universal (28:16-20). Prior to the new age the Jewish law was in effect (5:18), but with the coming of a "new heavens and a new earth" through the events of death-resurrection, that old law is replaced by the Torah of Jesus.[11]

Matthew, then, attempted to give perspective to some of the radical changes his community was experiencing by reminding them that the death and resurrection of Jesus had triggered the final age of salvation for which Israel longed. In this new age dramatic transformations were to take place.

A Two-Stage History

Another author who has given careful attention to Matthew's view of salvation history is Jack Dean Kingsbury in his book *Matthew: Structure, Christology, Kingdom.*[12] He reviews the opinions of some of the authors we have considered and notes that most of them come up with a "three-epoch" division of salvation history: (1) Israel, (2) the life of Jesus, (3) the time of the church, even though there are some variations on the precise demarcations of each period. Kingsbury also notes that for each of these authors the basis of division is some ecclesial concern. For Walker, it is the beginning of the Gentile mission; for Strecker it is ethical concerns; for Meier it is the abrogation of law and the shift in the church's mission.

Kingsbury himself goes in another direction. He believes that Matthew has only a "two-epoch" division of salvation history: (1) a time of Israel which is "preparatory to and prophetic of the coming of the messiah" and (2) the time of Jesus "in which the time of Israel finds its fulfillment and which, from the vantage point of Matthew's day, extends from the beginning of the ministry of John and Jesus (past) through the post-Easter time (present) to the coming consummation of the age (future)."[13] Kingsbury believes that Matthew has constructed his two-stage schema of salvation history not on ecclesial grounds but on the basis of Christology.

To support his thesis, Kingsbury points to evidence in the gospel which shows that Matthew considered his community to be in essential continuity with the period begun with the advent of Jesus. What is constitutive of this period of salvation history is the abiding presence of Jesus. Matthew affirms this at the very beginning of the gospel where Jesus is named "Emmanuel—God-with-us" (1:23), as well as at the end when the risen Christ promises his continual presence with his apostles (28:20). This shows that the "time of Jesus" extends "from his birth to the parousia."[14]

Other features of Matthew bolster this schema, according to Kingsbury. The time of the church is only a "substage" of the time of Jesus, not a separate epoch. In contrast to Luke, Matthew has no ascension account nor does he have a developed theology of the Spirit. This is because for Matthew the risen Jesus continues to abide in the church (see 13:37-38; 18:20; 28:18-20). This is also reflected in the exalted character of Jesus as portrayed in Matthew. The Matthean Jesus is "worshiped" (14:33) and consistently addressed by the disciples as "Lord." In the same vein Matthew portrays the disciples as more "understanding" of Jesus (13:1, 16, 51) and as knowing and doing the will of the Father (12:49-50). All of this, in Kingsbury's view, shows that Matthew saw essential continuity between the time of Jesus and the time of the church. In the evangelist's schema, the decisive element is his Christology. The person of Jesus, earthly and exalted, has triggered a new and final age of salvation history, an age in which Matthew's church participates because of the abiding presence of the risen Lord in the midst of the community of faith.

Rethinking Salvation History

Two recent studies that take up the issue of "salvation history" in Matthew call into question some of the basic assumptions of these previous analyses of the gospel and serve as good illustration of the

contrast between redaction criticism and more recent methods that draw
on literary criticism.

In *Matthew's Inclusive Story*, a book that had originated as an Oxford
University doctoral dissertation, David Howell uses the methodology of
narrative criticism to understand Matthew's overall perspective.[15]
Howell suggests that one of the reasons scholars are concerned about the
notion of salvation history in Matthew is that they are trying to
understand how Matthew's readers—usually referred to as his
"community"—are included in the gospel narrative (hence, the meaning
of "inclusive" in Howell's title). Even though Matthew's story concentrates on the events from the past, the impact of the gospel is to give
perspective for the current readers of the gospel; they are to see themselves within the events and message of the story and gain understanding
of their own place within history.

However, Howell questions whether the notion of "salvation history"
is an adequate way of understanding how Matthew includes his readers
in the story. Salvation history, he observes, is a somewhat abstract
"history of ideas" concept that derives from early twentieth century
continental theology and was originally concerned with the development
of dogma. As such it may impose an external, preconceived framework
on the gospel and in the process overlook the dynamics of Matthew's
narrative.

In accord with the perspective of literary criticism, Howell believes
that instead of looking for vantage points outside of the gospel, one
should allow the narrative itself to establish the "world" of meaning for
the reader. Howell offers a thorough exploration of that narrative world
from the vantage points of the "narrator," the "implied reader" and the
major characters and events of the story itself. Within that narrative
world there are many signals or projections into the future (what Howell
calls "prolepses") which indicate that the reader is included in the world
Matthew creates, ranging from explicit references to the time of the
reader (e.g., the statements that false rumors about Jesus' resurrection
have been circulated "to this day"—27:62; 28:11) to predictions of
future events (e.g., persecutions that will be experienced in the
mission—10:16-23; 24:9-14), and a host of other more subtle and
diffuse indications. Through the rhetorical device of the narrator in the
story world of Matthew there exist two sometimes simultaneous

temporal levels or two "nows": one is the "now" of the past story that is narrated about Jesus and the disciples but the other "now" encompasses the readers as the events and discourses and sayings of the gospel are directed to them and their experience. The responses of the disciples, of the leaders and the other minor characters—and, above all, the exemplary role of Jesus himself—are all intended to have an impact on the reader. The message of the gospel is not a series of propositions or ideas embedded in narrative that one is to extract from the text; rather, by becoming immersed in the narrative world created by Matthew's gospel, the reader gains perspective on history and how one is to respond to the reality of God's presence in Jesus.

Howell notes that we cannot draw direct conclusions from this narrative world about the actual circumstances of Matthew's community, although it is probable that circumstances affecting the real author influenced the shape given the "implied author" and "narrator" of the text and, in the same way, one cannot immediately make conclusions about the actual circumstances of Matthew's original readers by determining the kind of "implied reader" targeted by the text although there probably is a link between them.

Another approach is taken by Amy-Jill Levine in her study entitled, *The Social and Ethnic Dimensions of Matthean Salvation History.*[16] As was the case with John Meier and other proponents of salvation history in Matthew, she wants to understand how to incorporate the restrictive sayings about the mission to Israel (10:5 and 15:24) into Matthew's overall perspective in a narrative that ends with a call to universal mission. Some scholars have attempted a solution by characterizing these sayings as originating in earlier layers of tradition, traceable either to an historical saying of Jesus during the period of his public ministry within the confines of Israel or to early Jewish Christian traditions prior to the advent of the Gentile mission in early Christianity. In either case, the problem for the interpreter is to understand how and why Matthew incorporated these anachronistic traditions into a gospel whose perspective is now universal. Hence, the various schemes of "salvation history."

But Levine believes that most of these solutions are inadequate. She begins with the conviction drawn from literary criticism that Matthew's narrative has its own internal consistency and that the restrictive sayings in 10:5 and 15:24 are as much a part of Matthew's own perspective as is the universal commission in 28:19. In addition, she utilizes the perspective of feminist and deconstructionist approaches which suspect that texts or traditions considered peripheral by traditional approaches may actually be more to the center. Finally, these perspectives prompt her to look for continuities and relationships within the gospel material rather than divisions and oppositions. Here, too, Levine's own Jewish roots play an interesting role in her reading of the gospel. She notes that by assigning the exclusive sayings of 10:5 and 15:24 to Jewish or Jewish Christian perspectives and the inclusive commission of 28:19 to Gentile perspectives, one implicitly casts Judaism in a negative light. In fact, within the gospel of Matthew, positive responses to Jesus and his mission are evidenced by Jews as well as Gentiles.

Levine believes that Matthew's historical perspective within the narrative world of his gospel encompasses two "axes": one is "temporal" and the other "social." The temporal axis refers to the chronological sequence of events: during his lifetime, Jesus respects the traditional elect position of Israel and first brings his mission to the Jews. With the death and resurrection of Jesus, however, that exclusive privilege is ended and the mission is extended to include the Gentiles as well. This extension does not, however, abrogate the prior mission to Israel; that is to continue even though the Jews are not the exclusive object of the mission.

At the same time there is a "social" axis running through the gospel. In this perspective, the marginalized or disenfranchised respond positively to Jesus while those at the center or in positions of power often respond negatively. This axis cuts across lines of race and gender. The Roman centurion of Capernaum who responds with faith to Jesus (8:5-13) and the Canaanite woman (15:21-28) have much in common with the Jewish tax collector Matthew (9:9-13) and the woman with the hemorrhage (9:20-22). The gospel seems to look more benevolently on those who are mobile and without a fixed position (e.g., Jesus and his disciples) than it does those who are securely fixed in positions of power (e.g., the religious authorities; Herod; Pilate).

Far from being an insignificant or anachronistic piece of the gospel narrative, the texts of 10:5 and 15:24, which refer to Jesus' mission to the "lost sheep" of the house of Israel, are one place where both the temporal and social axis meet. Jesus' initial mission is exclusively to

Israel in line with the temporal axis, but it is to the *lost sheep* of Israel in accord with the perspective of the social axis.

Levine concludes that Matthew's gospel has a strong social critique. "By directing his mission toward all those excluded from full participation in the religious and political structures, the Matthean Jesus indicates the structure the church is to take. Replacing the temple with his own abiding presence within the community, he eliminates the formation of a new spatial center which would necessarily require peripheries. In the church leaders are to be servants, and equality will be insured through the continuing critique of centers." [17]

Conclusion

As with the question of structure, so here too it may be that Matthew's overarching historical perspective was not as clear or consistent as biblical scholars would prefer. Did Matthew define his schema so precisely that one can determine whether his fundamental rationale was either Christological or ecclesiological? And could Matthew tell us whether his distinction between the time of Jesus and the time of the church formed two distinctive stages or merely that of "sub-categories" within one stage? Did the evangelist construct a narrative that had a dual temporal and social axis?

Perhaps for Matthew many of the important features singled out by modern interpreters were in play at once. He was guided by ecclesial and ethical concerns as well as by his Christological convictions. He saw both continuity and separation between the life of Jesus and the time of the church. What is sure is that Matthew's gospel ties the present situation of his Christians into the broad sweep of on-going sacred history presented in his story of Jesus. That history found its origin and its promise in Israel, beginning for Matthew with the patriarch Abraham and extending down into the messianic age. The person and mission of Jesus, particularly his death and resurrection, had brought that sacred history to a decisive new stage, one that continued into the lives of the readers of the gospel and would continue to the end of the world. The Christian faith of Matthew's community had led to radical changes: isolation from the synagogue, an influx of Gentiles, radical adaptation of the traditional Jewish law, harassment from both Roman and Jewish authorities, tensions and divisions within the community.

By recalling the flow of history, Matthew reminded his church that such tribulations were not death rattles but the birth pangs of the new age inaugurated by Jesus, an age in which death would ultimately be overcome and a new experience of community, including both Jew and Gentile and those pressed to the margins, made possible. Allegiance to Jesus the messiah meant not just radical changes but new life and new hope. His mission in which the community shared and his healing presence in their midst fulfilled the dreams of Israel and thus provided deep continuity with the past and energetic hope for a new future.

If the precise details of Matthew's historical perspective remain debatable, the overall thrust of his perspective and its pastoral purpose are clear.

4
Matthew's Use of the Old Testament

Introduction

Any careful reader of Matthew's gospel is struck by the manner and frequency with which the evangelist appeals to the Old Testament. Matthew connects numerous events of Jesus' life with specific passages from the Hebrew scriptures. Besides these obvious quotations, Matthew's story is full of imagery, subtle allusions and typology drawn from the Old Testament.

The Fulfillment Quotations

Recent studies of Matthew have turned their microscope on this aspect of the gospel, too. The most intriguing texts are the so-called "formula" or "fulfillment" quotations. These are ten (or twelve by some counts, depending on what criteria one uses) quotations from the Old Testament introduced by a stereotype formula stressing the idea of fulfillment and applied to specific events or aspects of Jesus' life.[1] Since these quotations are a unique feature of Matthew's gospel, scholars believe that this material can give us some information about the origin and purpose of Matthew's narrative.

The fulfillment quotations span the entire gospel, covering the events of Jesus' birth (1:23; 2:6, 15, 18, 23), his entry into Galilee (4:15-16), his healings (8:17), his compassion and gentleness (12:18-21), his teaching in parables (13:35), his entry into Jerusalem (21:5), his passion and death (26:56; 27:9-10). But even though the full spectrum of the gospel is touched, most of the fulfillment quotations are limited to the first thirteen chapters and especially to those passages that are most uniquely Matthean such as the infancy narratives of chapters 1 and 2. Note, too, that many of the quotations are from the prophets.

All of these characteristics feed into the current discussion of the fulfillment quotations. Three major questions stand out: (1) What is the text form of the quotations? In other words, did Matthew draw these quotations from the Hebrew Bible (thus showing his knowledge of Hebrew) and, if so, what version? Or did he use the Septuagint, the ancient Greek translation of the Old Testament favored by the Greek-speaking early church? Or did Matthew make his own translation? This issue can be decided, of course, only by a careful comparison of the Greek text of Matthew with the many editions of the Hebrew Bible and Septuagint known to us today. (2) A second question is that of the "origin" of these quotations. Did the evangelist himself select and shape them as he wrote his gospel? Or were they already found in a collection of Old Testament texts that had been applied to Jesus by the early church? Or did they have some other origin such as a collection of texts for use in preaching? (3) A final major issue has to do with the purpose of the quotations. Did Matthew incorporate them to prove that Jesus was the messiah? Or to counteract Jewish arguments against Jesus? Or is there a more positive theological purpose to their presence in the gospel? And is the distribution of the quotations within the structure of Matthew's gospel accidental or does it have particular meaning?

To illustrate some of the answers that modern biblical scholarship has given to these questions we will sample the views of several Matthean interpreters.

The School of Saint Matthew

One of the first major studies of this question in recent decades was that of Krister Stendahl, *The School of St. Matthew and Its Use of the Old Testament*, originally published in 1954 and appearing in a second edition in 1968.[2] Stendahl's basic goal was to study the Old Testament quotations in Matthew, but he placed that question in the broader context of a hypothesis about the setting in which Matthew's gospel itself was produced. He stresses many of those features that distinguish Matthew:

its ordered structure, with the inclusion of extensive discourse material; its concern with church leadership (16:16 and chapter 18) and church discipline (18:15-20); and its studied use of Old Testament quotations. In Stendahl's view these elements give Matthew's gospel the character of a "handbook" for church life. Such a "handbook" was the product of a "school," that is, a loosely organized "milieu of study and instruction" (p. 29). It was a "school for teachers and church leaders" with the gospel assuming the form of a manual for teachers and administrators within the church (p. 35). Such a school had analogies in rabbinic circles but Stendahl believed that the closest parallel may have been Qumran, the quasi-monastic center of strict Judaism that developed on the shores of the Dead Sea from 132 B.C. to A.D. 70. This brotherhood of Jews "acted as a school which preserved and expounded the doctrines and rules of its founder" (p. 31).

Stendahl contended that the "crown jewel" of Matthew's "school" was its use of the Old Testament to interpret the life of Jesus. In fact, this may be the closest affinity between Qumran and the school of Matthew: the way the Qumran group interpreted the Old Testament book of Habakkuk is similar in style to the way Matthew handled Old Testament quotations. For Qumran, as for Matthew, the Old Testament texts were not primarily a source of rules "but the prophecy which was shown to be fulfilled" for both the founder and his followers (p. 35).

Stendahl attempted to demonstrate his thesis by a detailed study of Old Testament quotations in Matthew. He found that in those texts which Matthew has in common with Mark and Luke the form is similar to that of the Septuagint, or Greek Bible. But in the fulfillment texts, or what Stendahl called the "formula quotations," the text form, although composed in Greek, is closer to the Masoretic or standard Hebrew text while showing "deviations from all Greek, Hebrew and Aramaic types of texts known to us" (p. 97). Stendahl attributed this to the creative work of Matthew and his school. "In distinction from the rest of the Synoptics and the Epistles with what seems to be their self-evident use of the LXX (Septuagint), Matthew was capable of having, and did have, the authority to create a rendering of his own" (p. 127).

The analogy to Qumran helped Stendahl explain this peculiarity of Matthew. The Qumran group applied quotations from the book of Habakkuk to their founder, "The Teacher of Righteousness"; they were convinced that these prophecies found their fulfillment and their ultimate meaning in this person and the community he founded. The quotations they used from the book of Habakkuk are a unique form, indicating that the Qumran group felt free to adapt and shape the text in the light of their convictions about its fulfillment.[3] This type of *pesher* method (from the Hebrew and Aramaic word meaning "interpretation") is what Matthew and his school exercised with the formula quotations. Because they were convinced that Jesus was the fulfillment of the messianic prophecies of the Old Testament, Matthew's school shaped and rendered these key quotations to fit the contours of their traditions about Jesus and his teaching. Thus the formula quotations, according to Stendahl, not only lead us to the strong fulfillment Christology of Matthew but also give us an insight into the structure of Matthew's community.

Notetaker for Jesus

Stendahl's basic thesis about a school setting for Matthew's gospel has not been widely accepted, yet his detailed examination of the text form of Matthew's quotations continues to be a valuable resource and a point of reference. In the preface to the second edition (1968) of his book, Stendahl himself noted that research since the time his work first appeared in 1954 suggested that textual tradition of the Hebrew scriptures was more fluid and diverse than he may have thought and that, therefore, he may have attributed more creativity to the supposed Matthean school than was warranted.[4] Other scholars have also called into question Stendahl's comparison of Matthew's fulfillment quotations to the "*pesher*" method at Qumran; after all, they note, the Qumran method is intended to interpret an Old Testament text; the quotations in Matthew, on the other hand, are interpreting the meaning of Jesus' life.[5]

More recent studies have gone in other directions. One of the most unusual is the work of Robert Gundry, *The Use of the Old Testament in St. Matthew's Gospel, With Special Reference to the Messianic Hope*.[6] Gundry studied not only explicit quotations of the Old Testament in Matthew but even more subtle allusions (an example would be the allusion to Isaiah 63:19 in Matthew 3:16 where there is reference to the "opening of the heavens"). He agrees with Stendahl that such a free form is found only in Matthew's fulfillment quotations. The quotations

Matthew shares with Mark are based on the Septuagint, but all other quotations and allusions in the synoptic materials have evidence of the same kind of "mixed form" as that in the fulfillment quotations.

This led Gundry to further challenge Stendahl's theory about a special Matthean school as the source of the supposedly unique Old Testament quotations Matthew used. Gundry insists that the practice of making one's own translation of Old Testament materials—rather than depending on the Masoretic text or the Septuagint—was more common in the early church than one may have supposed. The Jewish Christians were, after all, used to the rabbinic practice of "targumizing," that is, of free, interpretive renderings of biblical quotations and stories.

But Gundry pushes his case much further. He suggests that the mixture of Hebrew, Septuagintal (i.e., Greek) and Aramaic elements in Matthew's quotations "harmonizes perfectly" with what we know of the trilingual milieu of Palestine in the first century. The only adequate explanation is that the source of these quotations is ultimately Matthew the apostle. Matthew, an educated publican, would be equipped for this role. He may, in fact, have been a "notetaker" among the band of Jesus' disciples, recording events and discourses of Jesus, even the interpretation of the Old Testament that Jesus applied to himself and to his messianic mission. These notes, according to Gundry, would have been the foundation of the tradition upon which the synoptic gospels were built. Gundry holds that the gospel of Matthew depended directly on the Greek gospel of Mark (this accounts for the presence of Septuagintal Old Testament quotations which Matthew brought over from Mark), but the ultimate source was the raw material provided by the tax collector Matthew. Thus Gundry envisages a very early date for Mark and Matthew, somewhere around A.D. 50-60.[7]

The theological meaning of the Old Testament quotations in Matthew is also of importance for Gundry's study. Gundry synthesizes Matthew's theology under the label "messianic hope." Matthew's Old Testament quotations cover a broad spectrum of Israel's hopes for salvation. Each set of quotations and allusions draws on these basic images of hope: Jesus is the royal messiah, the Isaian servant, the Danielic Son of Man, the shepherd of Israel. He fulfills the role of Yahweh himself in saving from sin (1:21), raising the dead (11:5) and giving rest to the weary (11:28-29). He is the greater Moses, the greater

Son of David, the representative prophet like Jeremiah and Elisha; he is the representative Israelite and the true just sufferer of Israel.

Thus, by means of Old Testament quotations and allusions, a wide spectrum of messianic images and types find their fulfillment in Jesus. This interpretation, Gundry believes, was not merely the post-Easter reflection of the church. The validation for that reflection was Jesus' own interpretation of the scriptures in the light of his mission. This interpretation was faithfully transmitted by Matthew's notes.

The Fulfillment Texts and the Plan of Matthew's Gospel

The studies of Stendahl and Gundry concentrated mainly on the form and origin of the fulfillment quotations used by Matthew. The important work of Wilhelm Rothfuchs, *Die Erfüllingszitate des Matthäus-Evangeliums* ("The Fulfillment Quotations of Matthew's Gospel"), tried to appreciate how these quotations fit into Matthew's theology.[8]

Rothfuchs agrees that the text form of the quotations is mixed, a blend of Septuagintal elements with unique translations. But he disagrees with the theory of Stendahl that these came from the exegetical work of a school. He also challenges the proposal of Georg Strecker that these quotations were part of a collection (or "testimonial") of Old Testament quotations used in the early church to prove Jesus' messianic identity. Strecker claimed that the citations in Matthew did not really reflect the evangelist's style, and the quotations give the impression of being forced into the text without an intrinsic relationship to the surrounding context. For example, the quotation from 2 Chronicles 29:30 in Matthew 13:35 speaks of revelation: "I will open my mouth in parables. I will utter what has been hidden since the foundation of the world." Yet, Strecker points out, Matthew uses the term "parable" in a negative sense in this chapter, as a vehicle not of revelation but of concealment for those who reject Jesus: "This is why I speak to them in parables, because seeing they do not see, and hearing they do not hear, nor do they understand" (13:13). This shows that the formula quotation is out of step with its context and was imported by the evangelist from a pre-existing collection of quotations. The only function of the Old Testament quotations for Matthew is to stress the "fact" of Jesus' life; the citations are part of a historicizing tendency in Matthew.[9]

But Rothfuchs disagrees on almost all counts. He insists that a careful study of the form of the quotations and their introductory formulas show that they are integrated with the evangelist's style and perspective, and that their purpose is more theological than Strecker thinks. One factor to keep in mind is the context in which these quotations appear. In the case of Matthew 13:35, for example, it is true that the parables are referred to as veiled speech for those who reject Jesus. But more of the context has to be taken into account. A turning point in the chapter occurs in 13:36, immediately after the Old Testament quotation: Jesus leaves the crowd and teaches the disciples privately in a house. According to Rothfuchs and others, this divides the discourse and, in fact, is a watershed for the whole gospel story.[10] Prior to 13:36 Jesus had spoken to all of Israel and, especially beginning with chapter 11, had experienced misunderstanding and rejection. From now on his mission is turned away from his opponents to the community of the disciples who do understand (13:11, 16, 51).

The fulfillment quotation accurately reflects this Matthean perspective. It is placed not at the end of the discourse but at the turning point after v. 34. Its content echoes the movement of the whole discourse: the first part, "I will open my mouth in parables," parallels the first half of the chapter in which Jesus directed parables to the crowds; the second half, "I will utter what has been hidden since the foundation of the world," coincides with the special revelation of the mystery of the kingdom which is given to the disciples and signaled in the second half of the discourse. Therefore, as this example shows, the fulfillment quotations are not bootlegged from some pre-existing source but were carefully integrated into the gospel by the evangelist.

Rothfuchs applies his redaction criticism method not just to individual occurrences of the quotations but to their distribution in the gospel as a whole. He notes that with the exception of 27:9-10 (the death of Judas) and 21:4-5 (entry into Jerusalem) the fulfillment texts are bunched in the infancy narrative of chapters 1 and 2 or, with the four quotes attributed to Isaiah, applied to Jesus' public ministry in Galilee (4:14-15; 8:17; 12:18-21; 13:35). These quotations, especially the Isaian ones, apply to Jesus' mission to the lost sheep of the house of Israel. Jesus carries out God's promised mission of salvation to his people.

This gives Rothfuchs a hint as to the origin of this style of Old Testament interpretation. It developed in the missionary preaching of the early church's mission to Israel.[11] The church's basic message to the Jews was that the promises were fulfilled in Jesus. But the mission to Israel had become a thing of the past by the time Matthew writes his gospel; now the mission is turned toward the Gentiles (28:16-20). So Matthew's Old Testament interpretation has a new purpose. Now it is the message of the community that the promises of salvation made to Israel and fulfilled in Jesus are, through his risen presence in the church, available to all people. This universal perspective is reflected not only in the explicit mission text of 28:16-20 but in the content of some of the Old Testament quotations themselves (see 12:17 with its quotation of Is 42:1-4).

Toward a Consensus

Each of the authors we have cited offers somewhat different answers to the questions posed at the beginning of the chapter about the form, origin and purpose of the fulfillment quotations. But the state of the art on this question is not pure anarchy. An article by the Flemish scholar Frans Van Segbroeck helps bring some order to the overall discussion of this issue.[12] His framework can serve as a conclusion to our review.

I. *The Form.* Van Segbroeck finds a good bit of consensus here. The thesis of Stendahl and many others that the fulfillment quotations are a mixed text form blending LXX, Hebrew and Aramaic elements has been sustained. Gundry has gone further, asserting that this mixed form is probably true of many other citations of the Old Testament in the gospels. What makes the Old Testament fulfillment quotations in Matthew's gospel unique is not their textual form but the way the evangelist applies these quotations to the life of Jesus. Scholarship also seems to agree that Matthew's quotations were formulated in Greek, thus indicating a Hellenistic church, yet one in close contact with its Jewish roots.

II. *The Origin.* Consensus is not as strong here. The "school" theory of Stendahl has not been widely accepted, nor has the conservative view of Gundry that these quotations come from the original notes of Matthew. Gundry's thesis also places the gospel of Matthew too early and compresses too radically the time span it would take for Mark's gospel to be formulated and for Matthew to be able to revise this gospel in his own format. Many scholars also believe that Matthew's gospel shows signs of being aware of the destruction of Jerusalem in A.D. 70, and of the changes taking place in post-70 Judaism, and therefore must be dated much later than Gundry suggests.[13]

Strecker's theory that the quotations were part of a collection or testimonial has not been given a warm reception either. Ironically, the discovery of the Dead Sea Scrolls proved that such collections were known in Judaism; prior to that archeological find the existence of such collections was merely a hypothesis. But most scholars are still not convinced that Matthew drew his quotations from such a source.

More weight seems to be given to the "preaching" milieu suggested by Kilpatrick and refined by Rothfuchs. "Preaching" must be understood in a broad sense to include all of the teaching and communication activities of the church's mission. In this context the early church probably developed a style of applying key Old Testament texts, especially from the prophets and psalms, to the events of Jesus' life, illustrating that he was the fulfillment of Israel's hopes. This process may have begun in the passion story but was soon applied to all of the events of Jesus' life.

This tradition of Old Testament interpretation, developed in the course of the church's mission among Jews, may well have been the origin of the style of interpretation found in Matthew's gospel. Graham Stanton and others have suggested that Matthew himself may be responsible for the particular form of the Old Testament quotations he uses. He notes that although Matthew tends to be a conservative editor regarding his sources, he does introduce some minor changes into the Old Testament quotations already found in Mark's gospel, adapting them to the context in which the evangelist will use them in his own gospel.[14] Virtually all scholars concede that the introductory formula itself is typically Matthean. Likewise, Stanton suggests, many of unique features of the Old Testament quotations found in Matthew reflect the style and perspective of the evangelist or his immediate sources rather than any specific text type.[15]

Therefore, while Matthew may have been prompted to use these fulfillment quotations on the basis of a tradition of interpretation in his community and in Judaism itself, the precise format of the quotations can be traced to Matthew's own editorial preferences, not to any pre-existing collection of quotations.

III. *The Meaning.* Writing in 1971, Segbroeck had observed that more work needed to be done in this area and more recent studies have taken up that challenge. Rothfuchs' book was one of the first major studies of the Old Testament quotations in Matthew from an explicitly redactional perspective. Yet Rothfuchs did not go far enough, in Van Segbroeck's view. For example, the rationale behind the distribution of the Old Testament quotations in the gospel might be discovered by realizing that chapters 1-13, where most of them occur, are precisely those passages where Matthew takes the freest hand vis-à-vis his source, Mark.[16] This reinforces the suggestion that the quotations are specifically Matthean and are important to his perspective. Van Segbroeck also suggests that the attribution of so many of the quotations to Isaiah is significant. Not only was Isaiah the premier messenger of salvation to Israel (a point made by Rothfuchs) but he was also the prophet who most bemoaned the failure of his mission. This, too, might be a reason for Matthew's use of texts from that prophet, since much of his gospel wrestles with Israel's rejection of Jesus and the Christian mission.

From the vantage point of his rhetorical study of Matthew, David Howell comes to a similar conclusion about the function of the quotations.[17] They fall under the rubric of "generalizations"—that is, appeals outside the narrative world of the gospel to a broader authority for the events taking place in the story, namely the authority of God through the Old Testament. These quotations are bunched at the beginning of the gospel because here is where Matthew introduces the reader to his perspective on Jesus. As the reader enters the narrative world of Matthew, he learns that Jesus' life and mission fulfill God's promise in the Old Testament; Jesus embodies the hope of Israel and thus his life and teaching are imbued with God's own authority. In the early chapters of the gospel, too, the focus in Matthew's story is on Jesus' mission to Israel and the first strong signs of the eventual rejection of that mission. The quotations from Isaiah that fall within chapters 4-13 help give broader meaning to that history. Thus overall the quotations present Jesus as the fulfillment of the Old Testament, as one endowed with God's own authority and therefore as a reliable source within the world of Matthew's gospel, and, finally, the quotations show the gravity of rejecting Jesus.

Ulrich Luz, too, emphasizes that the fulfillment quotations come early in Matthew's gospel not only because he is freer from the constraints of Mark's story in this part of the gospel but in order to direct the reader to the evangelist's point of view. Through these fulfillment quotations, Matthew emphasizes that the "life of Jesus corresponds from the beginning to the plan of God to which Jesus is completely obedient...."[18] Thereby Matthew also illustrates the movement of the gospel from Israel to the Gentiles who will respond to Jesus and the preaching of the community. In effect, Matthew asserts the Christian claim to the Bible in the wake of the conflict with emerging rabbinic Judaism. In the midst of this strong theological interpretation of the role of the fulfillment quotations, Luz offers a rather prosaic explanation of why the preponderance of the quotations are from Isaiah. Matthew may not have had access to the entire Old Testament, yet his library could have had a full scroll of Isaiah! Thus quotations from other places in the Old Testament may have been by memory.[19] Therefore economy as well as theology may have dictated Matthew's selection of quotations.

The contribution of recent Matthean scholarship on this issue demonstrates that the Old Testament quotations in Matthew are not mere "proof texts" or embroideries on the gospel story but an integral part of the gospel's message, placing the story of Jesus in the broader context of Israel's history and underscoring the messianic authority of Jesus. Although concentrated in the beginning and middle sections of the gospel (perhaps because of his interaction with source material), the quotations highlight almost every aspect of Jesus and his mission—his origin, his ministry of the kingdom, his teaching, his healing, his advent in Israel, in Galilee and into the holy city Jerusalem, his rejection, suffering and death. In all of this, God's promises of salvation to Israel were being fulfilled and embodied in Jesus, and this conviction—proclaimed in concert with the Hebrew scriptures—is what Matthew's gospel wished to proclaim.

5
Matthew's Attitude to the Law

Introduction

No single facet of Matthew's theology stands on its own. That is certainly true of Matthew's attitude to the Jewish law, another focal point of current scholarship.[1] How the gospel understands the role of the law is closely related to many of the questions we have already considered: the evangelist's milieu and particularly the relationship of the Matthean community to Judaism, Matthew's perspective on salvation history, and his use of the Old Testament. The law question also catapults us into the areas of Christology and church, chapters yet to come.

It is important at the outset to state what is meant by "law" in this discussion. It refers primarily to the Jewish "law," that is, to the Torah or Pentateuch that functioned as the revealed word of God, and therefore as primary religious norm for Israel's life. But the law issue extends beyond this to include what may have been Matthew's reactions to the interpretation of the law as reflected in Pharisaic or other Jewish traditions. As we will see, the problem posed for Matthew's community was not so much the validity or value of the Torah as such, but the Torah as interpreted in the light of Jesus' own teachings.

There are many reasons why the issue of the law remains a major question in current studies on Matthew's gospel. This issue, more than most, helps define Matthew's relationship to Judaism. And discussion of the law issue also often reflects the perspective of the interpreter. The role of law in Christian life has always been problematical, especially for Protestant traditions where emphasis has fallen on the Pauline tradition of the freedom of grace over against the constraints of the law.[2] Some studies of Matthew take this contemporary issue as their point of departure.[3]

In any case, it is clear from the gospel itself that the law was an important concern for Matthew and his church. In a much discussed text unique to Matthew, Jesus states: "Think not that I have come to abolish the law and the prophets: I have come not to abolish them but to fulfill them" (5:17). A large portion of the sermon on the mount is taken up with interpretation of law (5:17-48). Controversies between Jesus and his opponents about questions of the law abound in the gospel (see, for example, 9:1-8, 9-13, 14-17; 12:1-8, 9-14; 15:1-20; 17:24-27; 19:3-9; 22:15-22, 23-33, 34-40); in some instances, Matthew will even alter a story from his source Mark, making it into a conflict over law (compare, for example, Matthew 22:34-40 with Mark 12:28-34). The biting invective of chapter 23 seems directed against the law interpretation of the "scribes and Pharisees."

There is no question, then, that the Jewish law and its interpretation were important issues for Matthew. The problem is to determine precisely what Matthew's views on the law are. Some texts of the gospel seem to move in contradictory directions. The Matthean Jesus is intent on not destroying but "fulfilling" the law (5:17) and commands fidelity to "every 'iota' and 'dot' " (5:18-19), but in the same discourse important provisions of the Jewish law such as taking oaths, the law of talion and divorce seem to be abrogated or radically altered (5:31-32, 33-37, 38-42).[4] The scribes and Pharisees are excoriated for their interpretation of the law, yet their authority seems to be upheld (23:2-3). The Matthean Jesus seems to freely bend or interpret the law to the priorities of his ministry (e.g., 12:1-8), yet he also lashes out at "lawless" ones within the community (7:23; 13:41; 24:12; in each instance the word *anomia* or "lawless," sometimes translated as "evildoers," is used) and constant emphasis is placed on the importance of good deeds.

Trying to fit these apparently divergent viewpoints into a coherent theological perspective has been an on-going struggle in Matthean scholarship. We will sample some of the solutions offered.

The "Two-Front" Theory

One of the first major redactional studies of Matthew's attitude to the law was that of Gerhard Barth in his contribution to the important book,

Tradition and Interpretation in Matthew.[5] His long essay of over one hundred pages is entitled "Matthew's Understanding of the Law."

The heart of Barth's thesis is that Matthew's attitude to the law gains coherence when it is seen in the context of the evangelist's milieu. Barth suggests that Matthew was carrying on a struggle on two fronts. One group was the "antinomians," Christians who dismissed the law; against them Matthew stressed the enduring validity of the law, emphasized the need for good deeds, and raised the threat of judgment. On the other front were the rabbis of Pharisaic Judaism; against their interpretation of law Matthew stressed the priority of the love command and Jesus' own radicalizing of the law.[6]

Barth admits that attempts to identify precisely the "antinomians" are doomed to frustration. He speculates that they were a group of Christians who apparently maintained that Christ had abolished the law and the prophets. To counteract this, Matthew stressed that Jesus did not come to abolish the law (5:17). These antinomians seem to have relied on their charismatic gifts of prophecy and miracle working (see 7:21-22) as sufficient proof of their righteousness, but Matthew countered this with an emphasis on good deeds and action in accord with Jesus' teaching as the only criterion for judgment (7:21-27). Barth speculates that this group was composed of Hellenistic Christians since it is unlikely that Jewish Christians would dismiss the law entirely, and we do have indications of charismatic activity in the Gentile churches.[7] However, Barth did not believe that Matthew was pitted against a Pauline group (as might be the case in James). Beyond this Barth was not willing to speculate.

Matthew's other front against the rabbis kept the gospel from becoming merely another version of Pharisaic tradition. While Matthew emphasizes that Jesus affirmed the validity of the law, the evangelist stands in opposition to Pharisaic interpretation of the law. As so many of the controversial stories of the gospel illustrate—particularly the debate in 22:34-40—the absolute primacy of the love command is seen as the distinctive emphasis of Jesus' mission. This, claims Barth, puts Jesus' teaching in opposition to the interpretation of Pharisaic Judaism because the rabbis, in principle, claimed that each demand of the law is as important as the rest. By making the love command the fundamental principle of interpretation for all of the law (22:40), Matthew's gospel parted company with the Pharisaic understanding of law. In this, Barth suggests, Matthew was faithfully reflecting the sayings of Jesus and Christian tradition, but no other gospel writer expressed the issue so forthrightly.

Similar views to those of Barth have been developed in other studies. Hans Dieter Betz, who has written extensively on the sermon on the mount, offers what many feel is a radical solution to the apparent contradictions in Matthew's perspective on the law.[8] The sermon on the mount, he claims, derives from a strict Jewish Christian group and is imported almost intact into Matthew's gospel but without being integrated into Matthew's overall theology. Unlike the rest of the gospel, the sermon on the mount has little, if any, Christology and takes a dim view of the Gentile mission. Betz is willing to identify the "antinomians" targeted by the sermon as Pauline Christians. The sermon's demand of rigorous fidelity to the law (e.g., 5:17-20) and its apparent antipathy to Gentiles (e.g., 5:47; 6:7) reflect the opposition of this Jewish Christian group to Pauline Gentile Christianity, with its accommodating view of the law. Betz's views about the sermon, however, have not been well received by many Matthean scholars, particularly his claim that the theology of the sermon differs radically from that of the rest of the gospel.[9]

Matthew: Moderator of Traditions

Written in 1972, R. Hammerton-Kelly's article, "Attitudes to the Law in Matthew's Gospel: A Discussion of Matthew 5:18," linked the law question with the turbulent years of the late 1960s.[10] Does law have a place in a Christian context? The author suggested that Matthew's gospel may offer some guidelines.

Matthew's perspective on the law is shaped not by opposition to antinomian Christians and Pharisees but by the attempt to moderate polarities in attitudes to the law within the Christian community itself. Hammerton-Kelly detects in the gospel three different viewpoints: (1) a legally rigorous attitude which insisted that the law of Moses continued to be valid with all its force; (2) a view (probably similar to Stephen's Hellenists in the book of Acts) which held that some of the law had been abrogated by Jesus, especially those parts which inhibited the mission to the Gentiles; (3) a view which held that the law was valid but that the authority of the traditional *halacha* or interpretation of the law had been replaced by the authority of the risen Christ.

It was the third view that Matthew himself espoused. The key issue, Hammerton-Kelly suggests, was not whether the law could be interpreted—this was already done in Judaism—but by what authority it would be so done. Thus the law issue is firmly linked to Christology. Hammerton-Kelly finds the justification of his position in the key passage 5:17-19, especially 5:18: "For truly, I say to you, till heaven and earth pass away, not an iota, not a dot, will pass from the law until all is accomplished." Here one can witness the combination and interaction of the various viewpoints expressed above. The text of 5:17-18, down to but excluding the final phrase of v. 18, "until all is accomplished," represents the rigorist attitude. The addition of this final phrase exercised a moderating influence on the original text. "Until all things are accomplished" refers, in Hammerton-Kelley's view, to the resurrection of Jesus, the turning point in salvation history whereby the authority of the risen Christ supplants that of previous interpretations of the law. This juncture enables Matthew to add the antitheses of 5:21-48 which, in fact, radically went beyond traditional understanding of the law. This new "righteousness" (5:20) represents Jesus' teaching on the law. The law remains valid, but only the law as filtered through the teaching authority of the risen Christ.

Therefore, concludes Hammerton-Kelly, Matthew's perspective on law was a moderate position, in between the rigorous Jewish Christian conservatives and the ultra-liberal Hellenists.

Writing a decade later, Robert Guelich followed a similar line of interpretation in his extensive commentary, *The Sermon on the Mount*.[11] He emphasizes the importance of reading the sermon in the context of the full gospel in which Jesus is presented as the messiah and Son of God who inaugurates the kingdom of God. The sermon's demands reflect this fundamental Christological perspective: "the...Sermon develops the rather radical implications that the gospel of the Kingdom has for those who respond, who become the new People of God" (p. 173). At the same time, Matthew tries to counteract two distortions of Jesus' teaching. By framing the demands of the sermon in the context of Jesus' ministry and teaching, Matthew wants to avoid the distortion of legalism in the church which could become absorbed in the details of the law without its fuller spirit. On the other hand, by spelling out the demands of Jesus in the sermon the evangelist also wants to counteract an antinomian attitude "…in which 'everything goes.' Ethical conduct becomes relativized or rationalized into nonexistence. Matthew's stress on righteousness involving both relationships and conduct commensurate with the new age, his emphasis on the necessity of doing the will of the Father as being a concomitant element of righteousness, reminds the church that the gospel of the Kingdom includes inherently the 'ethics of the Kingdom' " (p. 173).

Two assertions made by Hammerton-Kelly and others have been points of discussion in other recent studies of the law question:[12] First, that the apparently divergent viewpoints on law in the gospel are to be accounted for by assigning them to various layers of tradition; for example, earlier more stringent views on the law's validity are included in the gospel but modified by Matthew's own more moderate perspective. Secondly, Matthew's theological perspective is crucial to his understanding of the law, namely his community's conviction that Jesus' authority as the risen Christ underwrites a new interpretation of the function and even the content of the Torah.

Before turning to further illustrations of these perspectives, however, we need to consider another viewpoint.

A New Law

The classical stance of B. Bacon and others who viewed the structure and theological perspective of Matthew as a "new Pentateuch" had important consequences for their view of the law. Since Jesus was depicted as the new Moses, his sermon on the mount was considered the establishment of a new Torah, replacing the now invalid law of the former covenant. Jesus' famous statement about "fulfilling" rather than abolishing the "law" (5:17) meant that his new law fulfilled and effectively replaced the old. The stringent sayings of 5:18-19 about observing the least commandment and respecting every iota apply not to the Jewish law but to the newly established Torah of Jesus.

This viewpoint and the conception of Matthew's gospel on which it is based have not received much support in recent scholarship. Few contemporary interpreters believe that the complexities of Matthew's theology can be adequately expressed by depicting Jesus as the "new

Moses" or the new messianic "lawgiver" who simply invalidates the Jewish law.

However, the emphasis on the disjuncture between Jesus' teaching and the Jewish law has found support in some studies. A good example is that of Robert Banks in his article, "Matthew's Understanding of the Law: Authenticity and Interpretation in Matthew 5:17-20."[13] Banks does not agree with Bacon's Pentateuchal theory, and his interpretation of Matthew's attitude to the law is subtly expressed, but, in the final analysis, Banks subordinates the law's perduring validity to the new authority of the risen Christ.

An important element in Banks' position is the meaning of the term *pleroun* ("fulfill") in Matthew 5:17.[14] He argues that the meaning of the verb in literature roughly contemporary with Matthew suggests that *pleroun* does not simply mean to "realize" or "establish" or "complete." The most frequent and revealing use of the term was in connection with the fulfillment of Old Testament prophecy. Therefore, it not only means realization or "actualization" but has a further nuance of "newness" or "superiority." It is this range of meaning that best expresses Matthew's phrase, "to fulfill the law and the prophets," in 5:17. There is an element of continuity (the law pointed prophetically to Jesus), but also of discontinuity ("that which is more than the law has now been realized"). This attitude to the law, Banks contends, is also expressed in the antitheses of 5:21-48, where Jesus' teaching moves beyond the law.

Banks concludes that for Matthew the Mosaic law had a "prophetic and so provisional function" (p. 242). Matthew was concerned to depict not so much Jesus' stance toward the law but "how the law stands with regard to him, as one who brings it to fulfillment and to whom all attention must now be directed" (p. 242). Such a position, of course, would put Matthew on a collision course with Pharisaic Judaism.

In his book, *Law and History in Matthew's* Gospel (1976), and in a more popular version of that study, *The Vision of Matthew* (1979), John Meier related Matthew's view of the law to his theology of history. We will treat Meier's view briefly since we have already discussed his perspective.[15] The rigorist statements about the law's enduring validity (5:18-19) can be reconciled with what Meier considers de facto abrogation of the law (for example, on divorce, oaths, talion; cf. 5:30-42) because the death and resurrection of Jesus is a radical turning point in sacred history. The law was fully in force "until heaven and earth pass away," "until all is accomplished" (5:18)—but the old age has effectively passed away and a new one has begun in the apocalyptic events of Jesus' death and resurrection.

Similar to Banks, Meier sees the meaning of the word "fulfill" best understood in terms of prophetic fulfillment. The Hebrew scriptures find their ultimate meaning in the risen Christ; they pointed toward Jesus and find their destiny in him. Matthew, Meier concludes, did not envision Jesus' mission as the dissolution of the law and the prophets. "His mission has rather the positive scope of giving the law and the prophets their eschatological fulfillment, a prophetic fullness which rescinds the letter of the law even as it completes its meaning. Jesus is the Messiah who brings consummation, not the revolutionary who brings desolation."[16]

Law and the Total Context of Matthew

Prompted in part by the emphasis of narrative criticism on the total context of the gospel, more recent studies of Matthew's understanding of the law have emphasized the overall coherence of Matthew's theology on this point and stressed continuity with the role of law in Judaism.

Alexander Sand's book on this subject is entitled *Das Gesetz und die Propheten* ("The Law and the Prophets"); its subtitle, "Investigation of the Theology of the Gospel According to Matthew," indicates the broad scope of his study.[17] Sand's thesis attempts to account for the subtlety of Matthew's viewpoint on the law and, especially, to relate it to the practical "ethical" concerns of the evangelist.

On a most basic level, Matthew means by "law" the Torah of the Old Testament both in its character as the revealed word of God to Israel and as the norm and regulation for their life. It encompasses, in this most basic sense, the totality of the "handed on and written revelation of God." For Matthew the Torah in this sense remains valid; Jesus does not destroy it but fulfills it, that is, in the preaching of Jesus the will of God revealed in the law is freshly and definitively expressed (5:17). Matthew presents Jesus' attacks on the Jewish leaders not as questions about the validity of the law but as in the line of prophetic critiques of the leaders of Israel, when such leaders lost perspective about the priorities of the law. The

Torah is "not a uniform codex"; there are weightier commands that have priority, above all those enjoining love and compassion for the neighbor (22:40). These laws have priority over the cultic laws, as the controversy stories in Matthew illustrate (see, for example, 12:1-8, 9-14).

Throughout his book Sand emphasizes that the ultimate purpose of Matthew's discussions about the law was not to counteract the historical Pharisees (although this may have been an obvious influence). The scribes and the Pharisees and other opponents stand as a generalized portrait, similar to the opponents of the classical prophets, those whose interpretation of law and fidelity to that law were lacking. Matthew's primary goal was "paranesis" or exhortation to the Christian community itself. His concern was theological and pastoral: to emphasize the necessity of "doing God's will." Such was the intent of the Torah itself, and the preaching of Jesus had the same goal. Such obedience is to be gauged by its "fruits" (see 7:13-14, 15-20; 12:34). Those who fail to do God's will, substituting mere words for action, are liable to judgment (21:18-19, 33-46).

Another goal of Sand's book is to study the significance of the phrase "the law and the prophets" (Mt 5:17; 22:40) as indicative of Matthew's theological perspective. He notes that in the Old Testament there was already an intrinsic connection between the functions of the Torah and the ministry of the prophets: both, albeit in different ways, had as their goal the revelation of God's salvific will to Israel, particularly God's care for the weak and defenseless. Jesus' own proclamation of the kingdom of God definitively affirmed and newly interpreted what had always been the message of the "law and the prophets." Thus this phrase should not be taken as two divisions of the biblical literature but as a summary of God's will for Israel, now brought to positive fulfillment in Jesus' ministry to the outcasts and his proclamation of the love command. Jesus' emphasis on the love command as the supreme norm of the law and the prophets ultimately defines what is meant by "righteousness" (3:15; 5:20) in Matthew.[18]

Sand's contribution deals effectively with many of the complexities of Matthew's attitude to the law and correctly links this issue not merely to polemical attacks on specific groups of opponents outside or even within the community but to the pastoral and ethical teaching of the gospel as a whole.

In an essay entitled "Matthew's Understanding of the Law," Klyne Snodgrass offers a state of the question on this issue and then draws his own conclusions.[19] The key point for understanding Matthew's perspective is that the evangelist presents what he considers the teaching of Jesus on the law. That teaching was defined not only in the sayings of Jesus but in his ministry. Jesus' view of the law neither abrogated the Jewish law nor was it the same as that of his contemporaries. Jesus had shifted emphasis from the "holiness code" with its concentration on separation from impurity to the "mercy code" with an emphasis on human need and on the values of love and justice. Throughout the gospel this emphasis of Jesus is clearly presented in the conflicts with the Jewish authorities, in Jesus' own acts of compassion and mercy, and in his explicit teaching on the priorities of the law (e.g., 9:13; 12:7; 23:23; etc.).

This same shift of emphasis stands behind Matthew's typical connection of the law *and the prophets*. Within the framework of the Hebrew scriptures the prophets exemplify with particular force the Bible's commitment to justice and mercy, and this is Matthew's point in stressing that Jesus comes to fulfill "the law and the prophets" (5:17) and it is why the prophets figure prominently throughout the gospel.

The law, Snodgrass emphasizes, was not a uniform legal entity but a series of commands—some of them in apparent tension with each other and needing interpretation. Matthew provides what he considers the hermeneutical key to the meaning and priorities of the law, namely the emphasis on mercy and justice. The authority for that hermeneutical key comes from the ministry and teaching of Jesus. For Matthew Jesus does not stand in opposition to the law but provides guidance about its meaning. Thus a distinctive Christian interpretation of the law and demands for fidelity to the law are not irreconcilable within Matthew's perspective.

Dale Allison, Jr. in a recent study of Matthew's theology entitled *The New Moses*, as well as in the major commentary on Matthew in which W.D. Davies and his student Allison collaborated, also stresses the cohesion of Matthew's perspective on the law.[20] There is no inherent contradiction between the sayings about fidelity to the law in 5:17-20 and the so-called "antitheses" of 5:21-48. Contrary to many other interpretations, the introductions to the "antitheses" do not convey that

Matthew is pitting Jesus' teaching against the law or even against traditional understandings of the law. Each antithesis should be taken on its own and the meaning drawn from the context. In many instances, what Jesus teaches goes *beyond* what the law demands and can hardly be termed as "antithetical" to the law. Allison contends that Matthew presents Jesus as the "new Moses"; the narrative leading up to the sermon on the mount in chapters 1–4 is important, for it establishes the powerful messianic authority of Jesus. What is presented in the sermon on the mount and throughout the gospel is the "messianic Torah," one that stands in continuity with the Torah of the Old Testament but also one that in this final age asks a "greater righteousness" (5:20) of the disciples of Jesus. Thus the so-called rigorist statements about fidelity to the smallest part of the law are meant to be taken seriously by Matthew and understood, in the light of his Christology, as applying to the law as definitively taught by Jesus.

As he consistently does, Ulrich Luz in his commentary on Matthew's gospel also finds that Christology is the key to Matthew's understanding of law and the rationale for the coherence of the gospel's statements about the law.[21] He, too, affirms that there is no contradiction among the various elements of Matthew's perspective on the law, nor does one have to resort to the somewhat improbable solution of having the evangelist incorporating into his gospel rigorist sayings about fidelity to the law with which he does not agree. In fact, Luz considers 5:17-19, with its emphasis on Jesus' fulfillment of the law and the exhortation to fidelity to every command of the law, as a necessary preamble to Jesus' distinctive teachings of 5:21-48. Thereby Matthew wanted to demonstrate that the teaching of Jesus should not be understood as abrogating the law or correcting it. Rather, through his authority as messiah, Jesus teaches the ultimate intent and meaning of the law and thereby stands in radical continuity with the revelation of God's will in the law and the prophets.

Luz sees an important parallel between Matthew's material on the law and his use of the fulfillment texts. In both instances, Matthew lays claim on behalf of his Christian community to authentic Jewish tradition. Through the fulfillment texts he shows that the predictions of the Old Testament find their ultimate meaning in Jesus; through the sermon on the mount and the other gospel texts on the law, Matthew demonstrates that the Torah, too, finds its authentic expression in the teaching of Jesus—and, by implication, not in the claims of his Jewish opponents.[22]

Conclusion

The law question has taken us deeply into Matthew's gospel. While many points continue to be debated, there are some important lines of convergence, particularly in most recent studies of the issues: (1) The law issue is not simply a matter of Matthew's struggle against outside opponents (for example, the synagogue) or even a particular faction within the church (for example, Pauline Christians or some kind of antinomian group) but goes to the heart of Matthew's message as a whole. (2) The law issue is closely linked to Matthew's Christology: Jesus' authority as the messiah and Son of God underwrites Matthew's distinctive interpretation of the law even when it seems to diverge from traditional interpretations; (3) Apparent contradictions between texts in Matthew that insist on rigorous fidelity to the smallest demands of the law and other passages where some commands are subordinated to others or even seem to be put aside need not be explained solely by postulating the presence of different layers of tradition in Matthew's gospel but by his overarching theological perspective.

6
Matthew's Christology

Introduction

Every aspect of Matthew's theology is ultimately connected with his convictions about the identity and meaning of Jesus. This should be evident from the topics we have already considered: Matthew's schema of salvation history, no matter how interpreters outline it, pivots around the Jesus event; Matthew's interpretation of the Old Testament scriptures is controlled by his conviction about Jesus' identity as the messiah; again, no matter how one interprets the fine points, it remains true that the role of law in Matthew's perspective is essentially linked to the authority of the risen Christ; and "righteousness" is now defined as fidelity to the teaching of Jesus.

Our goal in this chapter is not to attempt a comprehensive treatment of Christology in Matthew—a step that might have us tread ground we have already covered—but to sample recent scholarship on select issues in Matthew's portrayal of Jesus

Titles Applied to Jesus

Any student of the New Testament is aware that titles such as Son of God, Christ, Lord, etc., were important expressions of early Christological reflection.[1] One of the most comprehensive studies of Matthew's use of titles for Jesus has been the work of Jack Dean Kingsbury, primarily in his book, *Matthew: Structure, Christology, Kingdom*, but also in a series of more recent studies using the methodology of literary criticism.[2] Kingsbury examines each of the major titles in Matthew and attempts to establish some hierarchy and interrelationship among them.

The pre-eminent title in Matthew's Christology, Kingsbury claims, is "Son of God." This is the one title that occurs in every major section of the gospel and correlates with essential features of Matthew's overall theology. In the opening section of the narrative, 1:1–4:16, the first explicit designation of Jesus as "Son" is at the baptism in 3:17, but Matthew has prepared for this in the infancy narratives of chapters 1–2. The virginal conception insures that Jesus' origin is from God (1:18-20); he is "Emmanuel," "God-with-us" (1:23) and "savior" (1:21)—all indications of his status as Son of God. Kingsbury believes that the references to "the child" and "the child and his mother" (2:11, 13-14, 20-21) also allude to Jesus' divine sonship. The title is not explicitly applied to Jesus until 3:7 (although see 2:15 where "my son" is used in the quote from Hosea 11:1) because Jesus' identity as Son of God is a revelation from the Father, a revelation that points to the deepest mystery of Jesus' existence.

The title's presence continues in key moments throughout the gospel. Kingsbury admits that in the long section 4:17 to 10:42 it occurs only once (8:29); the main reason for this, he believes, is that the Son of God title is a confessional title, not to be used in a "public" or non-confessional way. The demon's use of the title in 8:29 is a valid exception because supernatural beings understand who Jesus is. However, even in this section, Kingsbury finds hints of the Son of God designation for Jesus. He teaches on the mountain (5:1), a place of revelation, of communication with the divine, and of authority. In chapters 5–7 Jesus is depicted as authoritative teacher; in 8–9, as powerful healer. The disciples Jesus chooses and empowers for mission are designated "sons of God" (5:9) or "sons of your heavenly Father" (5:45). All of these texts show that Jesus' identity as Son of God is a capital point for Matthew even when the title is not cited.

In subsequent sections of the gospel, important and explicit "Son of God" texts emerge. In 11:25-27 Jesus designates himself as Son. The disciples dramatically confess Jesus as Son of God after he appears to them walking on the waters of the lake (14:33). Peter does the same at Caesarea Philippi (16:13-20). In the transfiguration story, the confessional and revelational aspects of the title are again evident as the voice from heaven declares Jesus as "my beloved Son" (17:1-8). The saying of Jesus about being "in the midst" of the disciples (18:20) recalls the Emmanuel text of 1:23. The parable of the wicked tenants (21:33-46) who kill the son sent as messenger and the parable of the great supper a king gives for his son (22:1-10) again pick up the motif. The title also plays a significant role in the passion story: Jesus prays "my Father" in Gethsemane (26:39, 42); the charge of the high priest centers around Jesus' identity as "Son of God" (26:63). The title is especially prominent at the climactic death scene: the mockers challenge Jesus' identity as "Son of God" (27:40, 43), and in response to Jesus' death and the marvelous signs that accompany it (27:51-53), the centurion and his companions solemnly confess: "Truly this was the Son of God" (27:54).

Even though there is no explicit use of the title in the concluding scene of the gospel (28:16-20), Kingsbury believes that a Son of God Christology is operative there, too. The reference to Jesus' authority in 28:18 points to his identity as the risen Son of God, an authority challenged in mockery at the crucifixion but now vindicated through resurrection. Kingsbury finds many connections between this final commission scene and other key passages in which the Son of God title had appeared. It is on a mountain (compare 17:1-8), and there is a reference to the doubt of the disciples (compare 14:31-33), a reference to baptism (compare 3:16-17), and the promise of abiding presence (as in 1:23).

Therefore, Matthew portrays Jesus as Son of God from start to finish. It is a title that touches all aspects of Jesus' ministry and confirms his divine authority.

Although Kingsbury focuses on the Son of God title he does not ignore other important titles in Matthew. "Son of David" is one of Matthew's favorites (he applies it to Jesus ten times, compared with four each in Mark and Luke).[3] This title stresses Jesus' role as the Davidic messiah sent to Israel and also serves to focus on the guilt of Israel for not accepting him. Matthew signals this by having Jesus perform healing acts for outcasts such as the blind, the lame, and the Gentiles. These insignificant people acclaim Jesus as "Son of David" (cf. 21:5; 15:21-22) while Israelites reject him. But ultimately the Son of David title is subordinate to and redefined by Jesus' identity as Son of God.

This latter title also has messianic meaning in Israel, but in Matthew's gospel its connotation goes beyond mere messianic identity for Jesus.

"Son of Man" is also an important title in Matthew, as it is in Mark. But Kingsbury feels it is subordinate to the Son of God title. The Son of Man title is "public" in character, that is, "it serves to describe Jesus in terms of his relationship to the world, Israel first and then the Gentiles, and especially as he interacts with the crowds and his opponents."[4] In contrast to such titles as Son of God and Son of David which Kingsbury considers "confessional" titles, Son of Man is really a "technical term." Taking its basic literal meaning as "this man" Kingsbury suggests that it in fact does not divulge the true identity of Jesus. This self-designation of Jesus, "this man," is used in reference to the outside world to call attention to the authority God has given him—e.g., to forgive sins (9:6) or to have authority over the sabbath (12:8)—and to underscore both the opposition Jesus will endure and the future vindication God will give him.[5] As already illustrated, Kingsbury sees the Son of God title, by contrast, as a confessional title in Matthew, conveying what for the believing church is the "deepest mystery concerning the person of Jesus: his origin is in God and therefore it is in him that God dwells with his people.... As the Son of God, Jesus presides over and resides in his Church until the end of the age, at which time he will confront both Church and world as, again, the Son of Man."[6]

Kingsbury studies all of the major titles in Matthew, but we will report his comments on only one other, that of "Lord" (*Kyrios*). Some scholars contend that this is Matthew's most significant title, but Kingsbury disagrees.[7] He concedes that it is an important title in the gospel attributing "an exalted station to Jesus and one that is specifically divine," as in 12:8 where Jesus is declared "Lord of the Sabbath."[8] But the title cannot claim first rank because in almost all instances "Lord" refers to the authority Jesus bears precisely on the basis of some further designation such as "Son of Man," "Son of David," or "Son of God." For example in 24:42 the community is warned that in the final days "your Lord is coming." But this authority as "Lord" derives from Jesus' designation as the Son of Man who will come in judgment (cf. 24:37, 39, 44). The same kind of relationship exists with the Son of God title: in 14:28 and 30 Peter appeals to Jesus for power to walk on the water and to be saved when he begins to sink, but this authority of Jesus is based on his identity as Son of God as the confession at the end of the scene reveals (14:33). Therefore, Kingsbury concludes, the "Lord" title is "derivative," pointing beyond itself to more definitive Christological terms.

Kingsbury's treatment of titles in Matthew is thorough and coherent but has had a mixed reception among scholars. Some feel that he presses too hard for a comprehensive pattern in Matthew's use of titles for Jesus. Many would agree that "Son of God" is a key title and Kingsbury deserves credit for stressing its importance. But overemphasis on this title may devalue other theological categories in Matthew.[9] In an article entitled "Son and Servant: An Essay on Matthean Christology," David Hill, for example, criticizes Kingsbury on this very point.[10] He contends that in some major sections of the gospel the image of "Servant of Yahweh" shapes Matthew's concept of Jesus as Son of God. Servant typology was important to Matthew as the long quote from Isaiah 42:1-4 in Mt 12:17-21 demonstrates.[11] The qualities of meekness and compassion exemplified by the servant are essential qualities of Jesus' own messiahship.[12]

Other scholars have questioned whether the relationship between the Son of God and Son of Man titles in Matthew is that of confessional versus a public or "technical term," with the Son of Man in a subordinate position. A direct challenge on this score came from John Meier who dialogues with Kingsbury's position in his book, *The Vision of Matthew*.[13] First of all Meier is convinced that it is a Son of Man Christology which influences the final scene of the gospel (28:16-20). An important clue is 28:18 ("all authority on heaven and earth has been given to me"); this text appears to be an allusion to Daniel 7:13, a passage that refers to the future coming of a mysterious "Son of Man" (see also Mt 26:64 where the Daniel text is cited). The triumphant meeting between the risen Christ and his disciples in 28:16-20 is, in Meier's phrase, a "proleptic parousia," an anticipation of the final coming of the Son of Man in judgment at the end of the world (cf. Mt 24:30). The Son of Man has, in one sense, already come to his community to empower them for mission and to be with them until the end of time.

Meier further contends that Son of Man Christology plays a positive role in the rest of Matthew's gospel; it is not reserved to merely public, non-confessional contexts or reserved only for future judgment. The title occurs some thirty times (Son of God occurs only nine times plus three times as "my Son" uttered by God), in contexts that span the full range of gospel events: Jesus' servanthood (20:28), his authority to forgive sins (9:6), as friend of sinners (11:19), as "Lord of the sabbath" (12:8), as suffering, dying and rising servant (17:12, 22; 20:18, 26:2), as final judge coming in glory (10:23; 13:41; 16:27-28; 19:28; 24:27, 30, 37, 39, 44; 25:31). It is a title with a significance of its own for Matthew and should not be "swallowed up" by the "Son of God" title.

Meier makes a further suggestion: we should not think of any title as the central one. Both Son of God and Son of Man titles are important to Matthew. Perhaps when the gospel refers to Jesus simply as "the Son," the evangelist had in mind Jesus' dual identity as Son of God (with its messianic and transcendent dimension) and Son of Man (with its emphasis on suffering, compassion, and final victorious judgment). In this issue, as in some others we have considered, gospel interpretation may be best served when the interpreter does not demand too much systematization from the gospel writer.

Graham Stanton agrees with Meier that no single title holds the key to all of Matthew's Christology. In his work, *A Gospel for a New People*, Stanton considers the important, but somewhat neglected, role of the title "Son of David" in Matthew.[14] Matthew uses this title nine times in his gospel (compared to only three in Mark).[15] One of these comes in the opening line of the gospel, indicating the importance of the title for Matthew. In several instances, Son of David is used in connection with Jesus' ministry of healing (four of the six uniquely Matthean uses of the title). But another important connection is with conflict. Acknowledgment of Jesus as "Son of David" provokes hostility on the part of the religious leaders (see, for example, 2:3; 9:27-28; 12:23; 21:9, 15). Stanton believes that this controversy indicates we are "in contact with claims and counterclaims being made at the time Matthew wrote" his gospel (p. 185). In other words, through the gospel narrative, Matthew prepares his readers for the opposition they will encounter to their claims that Jesus is the Davidic messiah. And, at the same time, the passages in which the "Son of David" title occurs present a portrayal of the messiah that differs from current expectations: thus the child Jesus is the "king of the Jews" (2:2-6); he is a healer (8:17), one who is meek and lowly (11:29), the servant of God (12:17-21) and a humble king (21:5).

Stanton goes on to connect this distinctive Christology of Matthew to what he calls the "two parousia" schema which enabled early Christians to counteract the arguments of their opponents. The humble Jesus who has first come as messiah will be followed by his second coming as triumphant Lord. By implication, Matthew teaches his own community that they, too, must live humbly in the pattern of Jesus in anticipation of future vindication.

A study by Bruce J. Malina and Jerome H. Neyrey, entitled *Calling Jesus Names*, might also be cited here, although its approach is far different from the other use of titles we have been considering.[16] Utilizing methods and models drawn from social sciences and cultural anthropology, Malina and Neyrey explore what they call a "Christology from the side," that is, examining some of the titles applied to Jesus not so much for their theological significance but as a window on some of the social dynamics of the Matthean community and how titles or "labels" function within that setting. They concentrate on the conflict material in chapter 12 of Matthew as well as the passion narrative in chapters 26–27. For example, labeling Jesus as having demonic powers, as his opponents do in 12:24, reflects the cultural milieu of first century Mediterranean culture in which witchcraft was an assumption and shows the attempts of his opponents to discredit Jesus and label him as deviant from the norms of society. Likewise, although Jesus dies what is apparently a shameful death in the first century cultural context, his followers use this as a catapult to proclaim Jesus as "prominent," a social strategy that reverses the attempt to categorize Jesus as deviant.

The work of Malina and Neyrey represents a pioneering attempt to use social science categories on the titles for Jesus; the need to relate this approach to the more traditional theological approach is apparent.

Christology Beyond Titles

Other scholars have studied Matthew's Christology from vantage points other than that of specific titles. Dale C. Allison, Jr., who, along with W.D. Davies, has authored a major commentary on Matthew's gospel, provides an exhaustive study of Matthew's portrayal of Jesus under the typology of Moses in his work, *The New Moses*.[17] While most commentators have conceded that Matthew's emphasis on Jesus as lawgiver and the discourse format of the gospel (particularly the setting of the sermon of chapters 5 to 7 on a mountain) as well as some features of the infancy narrative (e.g., the threats to the child by a wicked tyrant; his rescue through divine intervention; the connection to Egypt) suggests an allusion to Moses, Allison believes that this typology is more extensive in the gospel and central to the evangelist's overall purpose than many interpreters realize. He traces the important role that Moses typology had in certain parts of the Old Testament and in extra-canonical Jewish texts. By portraying Jesus as the New Moses, therefore, Matthew emphasizes for his Jewish Christian community important continuity with its sacred past and, at the same time, underscores the authority and distinctiveness of Jesus as the messiah and teacher of a new righteousness. "Both Moses and Jesus were many things," Allison notes, "and they occupied several common offices. Moses was the paradigmatic prophet-king, the Messiah's model, a worker of miracles, the giver of Torah, the mediator for Israel, and a suffering servant. And Jesus was similarly a suffering servant, the mediator for Israel, the giver of Torah, a worker of miracles, the Mosaic Messiah, and the eschatological prophet-king" (p. 275). Ultimately Matthew uses Moses' typology in the service of his Christology: "Just as philosophers wore clothing of a certain king in order to advertise their office, similarly did Matthew drape the Messiah in the familiar mantle of Moses, by which dress he made Jesus the full bearer of God's authority" (p. 277).

Another aspect of Matthew's Christology that has come under scrutiny is his use of Wisdom motifs. A pioneer in this area was M. Jack Suggs in his book, *Wisdom, Christology and Law in Matthew's Gospel.* [18]

The linchpin of Suggs' position is the hypothesis that Matthew used Q as a source. That early Christian document, Suggs contends, was itself influenced by Jewish and early Christian speculation on "Wisdom," the revelation of God to Israel as metaphorically reflected on in the so-called Wisdom literature of Israel (see such books as the Wisdom of Solomon, Proverbs, Sirach, etc.).[19] The Q document may have drawn on a now lost Jewish "wisdom apocalypse," a series of oracles describing Wisdom's mission of revealing God to Israel, the sending of her emissaries in pursuit of this mission, and Wisdom's withdrawal from Israel in judgment on their rejection (Suggs finds traces of such a Wisdom myth in Proverbs 1:20, 21, 24-31). In Q Jesus himself would be presented as one of Wisdom's rejected messengers; thus Q did not develop a genuine Christology as such but presented Jesus only in the light of Jewish Wisdom speculation.

Matthew, on the other hand, reinterprets Q, significantly escalating its portrayal of Jesus. Suggs focuses on only a few key texts. In 23:34-36, for example, Jesus himself is presented as "prophet and wise man and scribe" to Israel. The Q text which Matthew used as a source would have spoken of Wisdom sending Jesus; Matthew makes Jesus himself personified Wisdom, the revealer of God. A similar interpretation is detected in 11:2-19. The passage reviews the "deeds of the Christ" (11:2) and concludes with the saying, "Wisdom is justified by her deeds" (11:19). The parallel passage in Luke 7:35 speaks of Wisdom justified "by all her children." Luke's version reflects the original wording of Q which identified John the Baptist and Jesus as emissaries (i.e., "children") of Wisdom. But Matthew's changes identify Jesus as personified Wisdom whose deeds reveal God. In the latter part of Matthew 11 Suggs finds further influences of Wisdom Christology. Matthew 11:25-30 draws on a Wisdom hymn which is now applied no longer to the Torah as revealer of God (as in the book of Sirach) but to Jesus who is in communion with the Father and makes him known, and whose yoke is easy and light.

In these texts, Suggs claims, we have significant evidence that Matthew used Wisdom speculation to present Jesus as the personified Wisdom of God, a crucial step in the development of New Testament Christology.

Some have been reluctant to accept Suggs' view. Marshall Johnson in an article entitled "Reflections on a Wisdom Approach to Matthew's Christology" questioned Suggs' hypothesis about a lost "Wisdom apocalypse" behind the Q document and wonders if Wisdom speculation had developed such a full-blown myth about Wisdom's emissaries.[20] And what evidence do we really have that Matthew intensified Wisdom speculation in regard to Christ, since we cannot be sure of his sources?

Suggs' hypothesis about a lost Wisdom apocalypse is the weakest part of his argument, but other exegetes have supported his contention that, in any case, Wisdom motifs play a significant role in Matthew's Christology. In a study entitled, *The Testament of Jesus-Sophia*, Fred W.

Burnett presses on with some of the issues raised but not addressed by Suggs' groundbreaking study.[21] Burnett maintains that the entire eschatological discourse of Matthew 24:3-31 can be seen under the guise of Jesus as Wisdom. The discourse is Jesus'/Wisdom's final testament to his disciples (= Wisdom's emissaries) after his rejection by Israel (see ch. 23).

Celia Deutsch amplifies the work of both Suggs and Burnett in underscoring the importance of Wisdom symbolism in Matthew's Christology.[22] The traditional qualities ascribed to Wisdom in biblical and Jewish texts—Wisdom as revealer, as teacher, as prophetic, and as experiencing rejection—all find a place in Matthew's creative adaptation of Wisdom symbolism to Jesus and his mission. In addition, the Wisdom influenced text of Mt 23:34-37 which speaks of the rejection of the God-sent emissaries also helps the gospel both affirm the authority of Jesus' disciples and explain their rejection in the course of the Christian mission.

In Johannine studies it is generally agreed that Wisdom motifs were instrumental in enabling the evangelist to make a conceptual breakthrough in expressing his convictions about Jesus as pre-existent and incarnate Word of God.[23] However, while Wisdom motifs have surely influenced Matthew's portrayal of Jesus, it seems that this was not a dominant perspective for his gospel.[24]

Jesus as Healer

The dominant presence of the sermon on the mount in Matthew 5–7 and the other great discourses of the gospel, plus the gospel's concern with Jesus as interpreter of the law, leave little doubt that Matthew presents Jesus as the definitive teacher. In fact, the disciples are reminded that there is only one "teacher" and one "master," Jesus himself (23:8, 10).

Less obvious, perhaps, is the fact that Matthew also lays great emphasis on Jesus' role as healer. A groundbreaking and still important analysis of this dimension of Matthew's Christology is that of Heinz Joachim Held, "Matthew as Interpreter of the Miracle Stories," first appearing as a doctoral dissertation in 1957.[25] Held focused mainly on the collection of miracle stories in chapters 8–9, a section of the gospel long recognized as a significant unit. Held's extensive analysis not only yielded rich results for understanding Matthew's theology but was a model of redaction criticism.

Held affirmed what previous scholars had already noted: that in this section of the gospel Matthew groups and re-edits a string of miracle stories found in his source Mark (with the exception of the cure of the centurion's servant which was drawn from Q; cf. Mt 8:5-13; Lk 7:1-10 and several sayings). Matthew has framed the entire unit of the sermon on the mount (chs. 5–7) and the miracles (chs. 8–9) with two identical summaries (4:23 and 9:35) which stress Jesus' teaching and healing, activities illustrated in the intervening chapters.

Matthew's re-editing and reinterpretation of Mark's material are extensive. He radically abbreviates Mark's stories (compare Mt 8:28-34 with Mk 5:1-20), not haphazardly, but in order to expand or highlight discourse material. The end result is a threefold grouping of the ten miracles into three major sections, each of which stresses a particular theme: Christology in 8:1-17 (the power of Jesus to heal), discipleship in 8:18—9:17 (the necessity of following Jesus wherever he goes), and faith in 9:18–34 (Jesus' response to the "praying faith" of his community).

Although subsequent studies have gone beyond Held's work, all use it as point of departure.[26] Two examples of alternate approaches will have to suffice. As part of his continuing investigation of Matthew's Christology, J.D. Kingsbury has also analyzed chapters 8–9.[27] While accepting Held's basic conclusions, Kingsbury adds some qualifications. First of all, following the lead of Christoph Burger, he prefers to see a fourfold thematic division of the entire section: (1) 8:1-17 on Christology; (2) 8:18-34 on discipleship; (3) 9:1-17 on the separation of Jesus and his followers from Israel (this subsection is a refinement of Held's original three-part division); (4) 9:18-34 on faith.[28]

In line with his thesis discussed earlier, Kingsbury maintains that the entire miracle section presents Jesus primarily as the powerful Son of God. Even though this title is not explicitly used, the Son of God Christology, already proclaimed in the opening chapters (1–4), carries over. Kingsbury concedes that Matthew cites the servant text of Isaiah 53:4 in connection with the healing activity of Jesus (Mt 8:17; see also Mt 12:17-21, a quote of Is 42:1-4, which is again applied to Jesus' healing activity), but in such key texts as 3:17 and 17:5 Matthew combines quotes from the servant songs of Isaiah 42:1-4 with Psalm 2:7 which designates Jesus as Son. Therefore, he argues, the servant title is subordinate to Matthew's Son of God Christology.

Kingsbury also stresses the significance of the miracle stories for Matthew's theology of discipleship. The gospel presents Jesus as the powerful Son of God in the midst of Israel (8:1, 10, 18; 9:8, 33), healing his people and gathering disciples (8:18-22; 9:9). These chapters are meant to be a lesson for Matthew's church, setting forth "the cost and commitment of discipleship and ways in which they are distinct from contemporary Israel (8:18-22, 23-27; 9:1-17)."[29] Matthew's Christians are invited to approach the exalted Son of God present within the community and to express their need, confident of his divine power. At the same time, there is a motif of "guilt" latent in these stories. The sick and outsiders such as Gentiles frequently confess Jesus as "Son of David" in the healing stories, showing that they recognize Jesus' messianic identity in contrast to the religious leaders who do not. "Such healing," Kingsbury claims, "underlines the guilt that is Israel's in repudiating its Messiah."[30]

The Scandinavian scholar Birger Gerhardsson also examined the miracle stories in his book, *The Mighty Acts of Jesus According to Matthew*.[31] Gerhardsson covers the full range of miracles in the gospel, not only the collection in chapters 8–9, but other stories and summaries of Jesus' deeds throughout the gospel. He makes a distinction between "therapeutic" stories such as the healings which are generally on the demand of the sick person, are scattered throughout Jesus' ministry, and are directed to the people or individual "outsiders," and "non-therapeutic" miracles (an example would be the stilling of the storm or the walking on the water), which, by contrast, are more occasional, are not mentioned in the summaries, are done at Jesus' invitation, and are performed exclusively for disciples. Gerhardsson concludes from this that the "non-therapeutic" miracle stories have a more problematic historical basis and are probably to be located more within the Christological reflection of the early church.

Gerhardsson stresses the importance of the stories and references to Jesus' miracles for Matthew's Christology. The gospel uses this material to portray Jesus' "incomparable *exousia* (= power) as the healer of Israel" (p. 93). Rather than a Christology subsumed under and dominated by the Son of God designation (as Kingsbury insists),

Gerhardsson believes that Matthew's Christology was "many-faceted,"
a portrayal of Jesus "illustrated with many kinds of material" (p. 82).
Many titles appear in connection with the mighty acts of Jesus: "Son of
Man," "Christ," "Son of David," "Lord," etc. He agrees with
Kingsbury that "Son of God" is Matthew's most important designation
for Jesus. However, the title of Jesus as servant is not submerged by the
Son title but, in fact, qualifies Jesus' role as Son of God. He is Son of
God precisely in that he is humble, obedient and serving. The Son of
God title is not applied to Jesus in the healing stories whereas servant
texts are (see Mt 8:17; 12:18). Thus the therapeutic activity brings out a
dimension of Matthew's Christology which the exalted title "Son of
God" does not. In fact none of the titles is essential to the miracle
stories; the narratives themselves present Christology by showing
Jesus in action.

Beyond Categories: The Depth of Matthew's Christology

Our survey of what scholars are saying about Matthew's
Christology gives some idea of the gospel's extraordinary richness.
Frustration in finding the dominant category demonstrates
Gerhardsson's sage observation about the multifaceted perspective of
Matthew. The Jesus reverenced by his church could not be contained
even by categories as forceful as teacher, healer, Son of God, Son of
Man, Son of David, Lord, Wisdom incarnate or triumphant Son of
Man. The object of Matthew's reflection rendered all categories
inadequate. That perhaps is one of the reasons the evangelist portrays
Jesus by means of a story, a narrative in which Old Testament
reflection, Christological titles and vignettes of Jesus in action are all
blended to convey his experience of Jesus' presence within the
community.[32] At this point ecclesiology and Christology meet.
Matthew's Christology is, after all, not an exercise in abstract
theological speculation; rather his portrayal of Jesus is meant to be an
exemplar for the church.[33] And even beyond this, Matthew's extraordinary portrayal depicts Jesus with numinous divine qualities. As
R.T. France notes, Matthew's insistence on the authority of Jesus—
indicated in so many ways throughout the gospel including Jesus'
majestic teaching and healing from the mountain tops (see chs. 5–7 and
15:29-31)—the miracles of Jesus, his supernatural knowledge (9:4;

12:25; 22:18), his transfiguration (17:1-8) and, not least, his luminous appearance at the conclusion of the gospel (28:16-20) combine to make a powerful and profound Christology.[34] In so doing Matthew presents Jesus as a figure whose divine authority and mysterious presence goes beyond any fixed titles or categories.

7
Matthew's View of
Discipleship and Church

Introduction

Similar to the preceding chapter on Christology, a study of Matthew's view of discipleship and the church takes us into almost every area of the gospel. There is, of course, no systematic or formal description of church life in the gospel, no theological treatise on ecclesiology. Matthew's vision of what it means to be a follower of Jesus must be deduced from the character of his story about Jesus, the disciples, and the other events and players in the gospel drama. Matthew's story is a story from the past but its intent is contemporary to the life of the evangelist and his community. This ecclesial interest of Matthew is evident from features of the gospel such as the discourse on community life in chapter 18, the fact he uses the term *ekklesia* or "church" three times (16:18; 18:17), the only evangelist to do so, and the instruction of the risen Jesus in the concluding scene of Matthew's story that the "eleven" are to "make disciples" of all nations (28:16-20).

What contemporary scholars have to say about discipleship and church in Matthew has, in part, already been described in the preceding chapters. The discussion on the milieu of the gospel (chapter 1) gives some idea about the probable atmosphere and make-up of Matthew's community: an urban, prosperous, Greek-speaking church composed of Jews and Gentiles, caught up in the tension of a critical transition moment. The chapter on salvation history dealt with how Matthew situated the existence of the church in relation to the phenomenon of Israel. The chapter on Matthew's use of the Old Testament added further profile to Matthew's church: in the view of some scholars, a Greek-speaking church well versed in the art of biblical interpretation, a church that saw Jesus (and, therefore, the community founded in his name) as the fulfillment of the promises made to Israel. The chapter on law added further insight. Matthew's church was enough in tune with Judaism to stress continuity with the "law and the prophets" but found, in the teaching of Jesus, its authority and norm for radically reinterpreting the law. The Torah of Jesus as presented by Matthew's gospel stressed the need for "righteousness," obedience to God's will expressed in good deeds, especially acts of compassion toward the neighbor. Here some of Matthew's special portrayal of the disciples finds its basis. And, finally, the chapter on Christology discussed Matthew's portrayal of Jesus as the basis and norm for all Christian existence and, therefore, as the foundation for ecclesiology.

Therefore, issues of Matthew's ecclesiology can be found in almost every aspect of the gospel. Our goal in this chapter will be to consider a few remaining elements not yet explicitly dealt with.

A Theological Basis for Church

An important study of Matthew's vision of church was that of Hubert Frankemölle, *Jahwebund and Kirche Christi*.[1] Because he attempted a synthesis of Matthew's ecclesiology it may be worthwhile to begin our discussion with a summary of his thesis.

Frankemölle locates the keystone of Matthew's theology of church in the bond between the community and the risen Christ, a point few would contest. Matthew's model for this, Frankemölle contends, is the Old Testament covenant between Yahweh and Israel, especially as that covenant theology was interpreted by the deuteronomist and chronicler. Matthew's recurring phrase "with us" or "with you" is, in effect, a covenant formula expressing Jesus' bond with the community. In 1:23, for example, Jesus' very name is "Emmanuel, God-with-us." In 17:17 Jesus laments, "How long am I to be with you?" In 18:20 the formula occurs again, expressing the risen Christ's solidarity with two or three of his disciples gathered in prayer. Matthew's presentation of the last supper (26:29) and Jesus' prayer in Gethsemane (26:38, 40) add the key phrases "with you" and "with me"—both expressing the deep covenant bond. The concluding scene of 28:16-20 reaffirms the continuing presence of the risen Christ in his church. This latter text, by the way, Frankemölle sees as modeled on the conclusion of the Second Book of Chronicles (26:23).[2]

In these and similar texts of Matthew's gospel, Jesus is presented as bound to his community just as Yahweh was bound to Israel. This "covenant" is the source and norm for the community's existence. The reality of this new covenant answers the theological problem of God's fidelity to Israel. Even though Israel rejected the gospel, God is faithful in that he forms a new covenant through Jesus.

Frankemölle sees this covenant theology borne out in other elements of Matthew's portrayal of the church, especially his portrayal of the disciples and their mission. Through their bond with Jesus, the disciples are designated "sons" of God. (See, for example, 5:9, 45; 8:12; 13:38; 17:25-26; 23:9). This, in turn, establishes a deep bond among the disciples/church members. They are the family of Jesus (12:46-50) and their relationship as brother and sister must be expressed in mutual respect and compassion (18:15-35).

Besides such "individual-personal" concepts as disciple, Frankemölle also examines collective symbols such as "people" (*laos*) and "church" (*ekklesia*). In each case these are drawn from Old Testament sources (especially Deuteronomy) but take on new meaning in the light of Matthew's covenant ecclesiology. In Deuteronomy the term "people" referred to those made such by God's gracious covenant; God would remain faithful but the "people" were capable of rejecting God and disobeying the covenant. In 1:21 and 27:24-25 Frankemölle sees this polarity of meaning present in a new context. In 1:21 "people" refers to all, Jews and Gentiles, who will be offered God's gracious salvation through Jesus. But in 27:24-25 Matthew indicates that those who reject Jesus thereby lose their status as God's people. Matthew attempts to fit Israel's rejection of the gospel into a long-standing biblical tradition.

The term *ekklesia* or "church," according to Frankemölle, is also steeped in covenant theology. Matthew's designation "my (that is, Jesus') church" (16:18) draws its inspiration from Deuteronomy and Chronicles which speak of Israel as "Yahweh's ekklesia" or "assembly": the "church" is the faithful remnant that through fidelity to the covenant truly belongs to God's people. For Matthew, too, the "church" or assembly of God's people means those who accept Jesus as a new expression of the covenant.

Frankemölle relates almost every aspect of Matthew's gospel to this basic covenant model. The demand for obedience to the will of the Father, the law as newly interpreted and grounded by Christ, the mission to the Gentiles (a people capable of belonging to God's people through faith in Jesus), judgment on Israel and those who fail in this covenant obligation—all these aspects of Christian existence find their ultimate synthesis in Matthew's concept of the church as the new covenant community.

Not all would accept Frankemölle's singular emphasis on covenant as the major motif of Matthew's ecclesiology. If in fact the church so definitively replaced Israel, it would seem logical for Matthew to name the church the "new Israel."[3] But in fact Matthew does not go that far. While the covenant motif may be less dominant than Frankemölle suggests, many of the aspects of Matthew's ecclesiology he stresses are valid. Surely Matthew does highlight the personal bond between Jesus and the community, and he does see Jesus' mission as the fulfillment of the Old Testament promises. Likewise Matthew does present Israel's rejection of Jesus as a failure with historic consequences resulting in the inclusion of Gentiles (see, for example, 21:43). And, finally, belonging to Jesus' church does involve faith in Christ and obedience to the will of the Father as taught by Jesus. It is in these elements of discipleship that further insight into Matthew's ecclesiology can be gained.

Discipleship in Matthew

A number of scholars have offered detailed studies of discipleship in Matthew, and there seems to be considerable consensus about the broad features of this part of the gospel.[4]

Jean Zumstein attempted a more comprehensive synthesis of the issue in his book, *La Condition du Croyant dans L'Évangile selon Matthieu* ("The Situation of the Believer in the Gospel According to Matthew").[5] His treatment can help us review the essential data.

Zumstein's basic thesis is that through his portrayal of the disciples Matthew describes the qualities of Christian existence—a point few scholars would dispute. Matthew presents the disciples as a homogenous and specific group, distinct from both "the crowds," who form a neutral group and are the object of Jesus' ministry,[6] and Jesus' various opponents who symbolize those who reject Jesus.[7] The disciples are the privileged companions of Jesus and are defended by him. Similar to Frankemölle and others, Zumstein finds the theological foundation for Matthew's identification of "disciples" with Christians in the on-going bond of the risen Christ with his church. Texts such as 28:16-20, 5:17-20, and 11:25-30 affirm the continuing presence and authority of Christ in the community.

By closely examining various categories in the gospel, Zumstein believes we can add further coloration to a portrayal of the Matthean church. For example, favorable references to "scribes" suggest that they had a leadership role in Matthew's church as interpreters of tradition (13:52) and as ones responsible for mission work, perhaps among their Jewish brethren (23:34).[8] Prophets also played a role in the church, but a diminishing one after the catastrophe of A.D. 70 because one of their main responsibilities was mission work among the Jews (see 5:12; 10:41; 23:34, 37). At several points in the gospel there are hints of problems and tensions: "lawlessness" (7:23; 24:12), "scandal" (18:5-9), "divisions" (10:21), persecutions (10:17-23), etc. The church is a mixture of good and bad, of wheat and tares until the end of time (13:24-30, 36-43, 47-50).

Most of Zumstein's efforts are concentrated on the disciples as presented by Matthew. The Matthean disciples "understand" Jesus. This is a sharp contrast from Mark where the disciples often fail to comprehend Jesus (compare Mk 6:52 and Mt 14:33; Mk 8:19 and Mt 16:12). Matthew does not idealize the disciples; they are still capable of failure, but, much more evidently than in Mark, the disciples are able to penetrate the mystery of Jesus' identity. Such sympathetic comprehension of Jesus and his teaching is a quality of Christian existence (13:23, 51). The disciple is also expected to hear the call of Christ (4:18-22; 9:9) and to "follow" him (8:18-22), leaving behind his or her former mode of existence (10:37-39). The disciples, of course, must have "faith" in Christ, putting complete trust in him, especially in the midst of trial and crisis, a point frequently illustrated in the miracle stories (see, for example, 8:10, 13; 9:2, 22, 28-29, etc.). The disciple must also extend such confident faith to the future, waiting in active vigilance for the unexpected coming of the master (24:27-44, 45-51; 25:1-13).

A special emphasis of Matthew is the theme of "little faith," a term the evangelist discovers in Q (see Mt 6:3; Lk 12:28) but further develops (8:26; 14:31; 16:8; 17:20). The disciples have authentic faith but it is still weak and in need of development. The gospel recognizes that the world is a dangerous place which can provoke a crisis of faith, leading to the paralysis of "doubt" (14:31; 28:17) and fear (14:30) even as one believes.

As was noted in our chapter on the law, the gospel is concerned with what Zumstein calls the "ethical" response of the disciple/believer. The starting point of all ethical response, according to Zumstein, is the "gracious offer of eschatological happiness" (see, for example, the beatitudes of 5:2-12); the challenge for discipleship is "by what decision of life do I respond" to this gracious offer? Guidance for that response is found throughout the gospel in such texts as the radical teaching of the sermon on the mount with its call for "love of enemies" and being "perfect as your heavenly Father is perfect" (5:43-48), and in the judgment parables such as 25:31-46.

The "church" according to Matthew is, therefore, the assembly of those who respond in faith and obedience to the invitation of the coming kingdom (22:1-14; 21:33-46). The church is not to be identified with the kingdom; there are various levels of response as one moves toward the final consummation of history (13:36-43, 47-50). True greatness within the church is to be marked by concern for the weak members (18:6-14), by "fraternal discipline" (18:15-20) and limitless forgiveness (18:21-35).[9] At the same time, the community is to give to the world the witness of good deeds (5:13-16) and is to be involved in active proclamation of the gospel of the kingdom (10:1, 7-8) to all nations (28:16-20).

According to David Orton, Matthew communicates his vision of Christian discipleship not only through his portrayal of those characters who bear the title "disciple" but through another designation that has particular importance in Matthew's gospel, namely the "scribe."[10] From a study of the ideal scribe in Old Testament and extra-canonical literature, Orton lists the following general characteristics: (1) the scribe is a figure imbued with wisdom and understanding; (2) one who has authority as a custodian of the community's values and true righteousness; (3) one who does right teaching; (4) one who shows the insight and mission of a prophet; (5) one who creatively contributes to the life of the community through new insights and interpretation.[11]

This ensemble of qualities, Orton notes, also define the Matthean Jesus' description of the ideal scribe "trained for the kingdom of heaven" in Mt 13:52. Here as well as Mt 23:2 which affirms the teaching authority of the scribe and 23:34 which speaks of the scribes sent by God and experiencing the same kind of rejection as the prophets are indications that the ideal scribe was an important way of describing authentic discipleship in Matthew's community. Orton goes on to suggest that the evangelist himself may have come from the scribal tradition. In any case it is clear that in a number of instances the qualities singled out by Zumstein in examining Matthew's portayal of the disciple coincide with the portrait of the scribe in Matthew.

Another perspective on the question of church and discipleship in Matthew is developed in Michael H. Crosby's book, *House of Disciples*.[12] Crosby's purpose is not to trace Matthew's portrayal of the disciples or his notion of the church as such, but to articulate a Christian theology of justice in dialogue with Matthew's theology. He proposes what he calls an "interactive hermeneutic" that attempts to do for the contemporary church what Matthew did for his own community, namely illustrating the profound ethical implications of Jesus' teaching. A key to understanding Matthew's context, Crosby maintains, is the important social structure of the "household" within the first century Greco-Roman world. Matthew's community would be composed of "house churches," small communal units within the larger context of Roman society; the disciples were, in effect, members of the household of Jesus (see Mt 12:46-50). The challenge for Matthew was to help his fellow Christians understand how the teaching of Jesus would transform relationships within the household communities or even where two or three disciples of Jesus gathered, and, through them, challenge the larger world.

In this context, Crosby reviews Matthew's perspective on justice, on use of possessions, on authority, and on the need for conversion of heart if one is to live by the vision of faithful human life and the community of justice transmitted by Jesus (25:31-46). Crosby's work is a distinctive interpretation of Matthew's theology whose primary merit is to draw attention to the strong dimension of justice, including economic justice, inherent in this gospel.

Peter: Representative Disciple or Symbol of Leadership?

Another distinctive feature of Matthew's portrayal of discipleship, one with important implications for his understanding of the church, is the role of Peter in Matthew's gospel, an aspect of the gospel that has continued to command the attention of biblical interpreters.

A comparison of Matthew with his probable source Mark reveals that the evangelist has significantly inflated the role of Peter. Matthew retains such important Markan texts where Peter is the first one called (4:18) and the one who confesses Jesus (16:16) but adds several unique Petrine passages such as Peter's walking on the water (14:28-31), Jesus' special blessing of Peter (16:17-19), the story of the temple tax (17:24-27) and the discussion about forgiveness (18:21-22). While greater prominence is given to Peter, the evangelist does not gloss over negative traditions about Peter such as his attempt to dissuade Jesus from the cross (16:22-23) or Peter's denial (26:33-35, 69-75). In some instances Matthew portrays Peter in a worse light than Mark does (see, for example, the addition of the word "scandal" in 16:23 or denial "with an oath" in 26:74).

So the figure of Peter in Matthew's gospel is a "mixed" portrayal: a prominent spokesman for the disciples, blessed by Jesus, yet also fearful, weak in faith, an obstacle to Jesus, and capable of outright failure.

Biblical scholarship has been divided over how to interpret Peter's role in the gospel. Two main trends can be detected in recent studies. (1) Some see Peter's role as merely "representative," that is, Peter dramatizes the positive and the negative qualities of all Christian disciples. He does not represent anything beyond that, such as a type or symbol of leadership within the community. (2) Other scholars move in a different direction: they concede that Peter does serve as a "representative disciple" but believe that the strong focus on Peter indicates something more.

This issue, of course, has important ecumenical implications since Roman Catholicism has traditionally appealed to Petrine texts such as Matthew 16:16-19 as a biblical foundation for the papal office. Happily most exegetical studies of Matthew's gospel have moved beyond strident apologetics for later church positions, Catholic or Protestant. Few Roman Catholic scholars, for example, would construe Jesus' words to Peter in Mt 16:16-19 as simply tantamount to the installation of the first pope. And most Protestant scholars survey the biblical evidence on Peter without the object of discrediting the papacy (although the recent work of Arlo Nau, considered below, might be an exception to this). At the same time, however, the role of Peter in Matthew and in other New Testament texts may be important evidence for emerging structures in the early church, so contemporary ecumenical discussion cannot be divorced from exegesis of these passages.

We will consider the interpretations of several scholars, both Roman Catholic and Protestant, to help us see the state of the art on this issue.

In his article "The Figure of Peter in Matthew's Gospel as a Theological Problem," Jack Dean Kingsbury, a Lutheran scholar, holds the position that Peter, while an important figure in Matthew's gospel, is, nevertheless, a representative figure "squarely within the circle of the disciples."[13] Kingsbury sifts through all the data, noting the attention Matthew gives to Peter but finding that in each instance the evangelist ascribes to the other disciples the same functions given to Peter such as "binding and loosing" (16:19 and 18:18), being declared "blessed" (16:17 and 13:16-17), confessing Jesus as "Son of God" (16:16 and 14:33), and so on.[14] Kingsbury concedes one point to those who believe Peter has a special position: Peter enjoys a "salvation-historical primacy." Peter and the rest of the gospel cast are figures "from the past" as well as types for discipleship within the present of Matthew's church. In this salvation-history perspective, Peter plays a primary role as the first called (4:18) and as spokesman for the disciples. It is this "historical" role that Matthew expands in his story, in comparison with Mark. But this type of primacy does not put Peter outside the circle of the disciples; he is merely *primus inter pares*. The church in Matthew is egalitarian in nature: while some exercise different functions such as teacher (13:52; 23:8-10) there are no "offices." No one has rank over another (23:8-13); the entire community holds authority (18:18-20). Jesus as the exalted messiah and Son of God is the one who guides and rules the church (18:18-20; 23:8-10; 28:18-20).

In a work that originated as a doctoral dissertation at Fuller

Evangelical Seminary, *The Concept of Disciple in Matthew's Gospel*, Michael J. Wilkins, an Evangelical scholar, studies Matthew's use of the term *mathetes* and its relationship to the evangelist's portrayal of Peter.[15] Wilkins' method was to focus primarily on the meaning of the term "disciple" or *mathetes* in classical literature, the Old Testament, inter-testamental literature and, finally, in Matthew's gospel. His conclusions differ little from that of Kingsbury, namely, that the disciples in Matthew are meant to be exemplary for discipleship within Matthew's community. The evangelist's portrayal of the "historical disciples" also has in mind the Christian lives of the members of his own community. Thus Matthew portrays not only the vocation of the disciples and their blessings but their weaknesses as well.

Wilkins' conclusions about Peter in the gospel of Matthew move in a similar vein. Whereas the disciples are a group of virtually anonymous disciples, Matthew gives color and shape to his representational portrayal of the individual disciple, Peter. Wilkins seems to concede that Peter may also serve as an example of leadership in the community: "Even as Peter had success and failure as a leader, so the leaders of the church can learn from Peter's example" (p. 223). But Peter's leading role in the gospel story is "historical" in character; the figure of Peter does not signify any continuing office or structure of leadership within the Matthean church.

Another Lutheran interpreter, Arlo Nau, takes a much more radical stance in his work, *Peter in Matthew*, one different in tone and purpose from that of Kingsbury and Wilkins.[16] Nau reviews the "mixed" portrayal of Peter in Matthew, noting as most studies do that the evangelist includes both positive and negative elements about Peter. But Nau detects an uneven stance on Matthew's part. In most instances Peter starts well but ends poorly (as, for example, in the story of the walking on the water in Mt 14:22-33). The explanation of this, Nau contends, is a struggle within Matthew's community between those who coveted a more ecclesiastical authority structure and those holding out for a charismatic, egalitarian vision of the community. The ultimate purpose of the negative portrayal of Peter in Matthew's gospel is to contrast him, not with the other disciples, but with Jesus. In regard to Peter, Matthew's gospel is an "encomium of dispraise"—a form of rhetoric intended "to dishonor, to disparage, to cast blame or shame upon a rival or antagonist" (p. 137). For Matthew, Jesus alone is to be the sole authority within the community.

Nau's conclusions suggest that he is viewing Matthew's gospel and early church history from a decidedly anachronistic perspective. He states that the emergence of the papacy and virtually all institutional forms of church authority was a tragic and, indeed, sinful compromise of the original spirit of Jesus and the gospel. If the contemporary church is to free itself not only of ecclesiastical sanctimoniousness but also of the evils of "elitism, chauvinism, patriarchy, and defensive self-interest," then it will have to purge itself of its misunderstanding of Matthew's portrayal of Peter, or what the author calls "the infectious influence of the Matthew 16:17-19 syndrome" (p. 147). In fairness it should be said that Nau explicitly directs his critique to all churches. However, he cannot be unaware that such a characterization sets its sights squarely on Roman Catholics, and to speak of Catholicism's tradition of linking the papal ministry to Matthew 16:17-19 as an "infectious...syndrome" is unlikely to advance ecumenism.

Looking at the same evidence, other scholars—Protestant and Catholic—have reached very different conclusions. A significant study is the book *Peter in the New Testament*, an examination of all the New Testament material on Peter by an ecumenical team of scholars.[17] Raymond Brown, who was a Roman Catholic participant in the study, synthesized some of its results in an essay entitled "The Meaning of Modern New Testament Studies for an Ecumenical Understanding of Peter and a Theology of the Papacy."[18]

Brown and his colleagues agree with the conclusions of Kingsbury and others that in most passages of Matthew, Peter acts as a representative figure, exemplifying positive and negative features of Christian discipleship. And he would also agree that most of the powers attributed to Peter are assigned to the church as a whole. But there are distinctions seemingly reserved for Peter. Peter alone is given the "keys to the kingdom of heaven" (16:19) and called the "rock" on which the church is built (16:18). And even though the disciples have confessed Jesus as Son of God in 14:33, Peter's confession is singled out and he is individually blessed as having received a revelation from the Father (16:17). It is difficult to see how such emphasis portrays Peter merely as "representative," as Kingsbury and Wilkins contend, much less as the object of disparagement proposed by Nau's study. Also, Brown and his colleagues emphasize that the burgeoning image of Peter in Matthew is not limited to his salvation-historical role in the period of Jesus' earthly existence but, as in the case of the temple tax (17:24-27), has to do with the resolution of problems for the post-Easter church. Note, too, that in the story of the tax, a shekel is provided for Jesus *and Peter* (not for the community as a whole; see 17:27), another hint at Peter's singular importance.

Perhaps the most important contribution made by Brown and his colleagues is that they discuss Peter's role not only within the context of Matthew's gospel but within the New Testament as a whole. Here they detect a Petrine "trajectory" which attributes increasing prominence to Peter's image as pastor, missionary, martyr, confessor of the faith, receiver of special revelation, and guardian of the faith, and also as a weak and sinful man.[19] Elements of this multiple image are found not only in Matthew's special tradition about Peter but in texts as diverse as John 21, Luke 5:1-11 and 22:31-32, many places in Acts, and in the two letters written in Peter's name. A parallel sort of trajectory develops around Paul, as can be seen in his image as martyr, pastor, and guardian of the faith in the pastoral epistles. But the Petrine trajectory became the dominant one, and in 2 Peter 3:15-16 we have an instance in which "Peter" is presented as the authentic interpreter of Pauline tradition. The full development of the Petrine trajectory takes us beyond the New Testament into early patristic writings.

In his own essay, Brown suggests that it is not so much an individual piece of the Petrine tradition such as in Matthew's Gospel which bears crucial ecumenical implications as it is the development of the Petrine trajectory throughout the New Testament in which Matthew's text plays an important part. The trajectory itself may give us a better idea of the emerging ecclesial consciousness of early Christianity, and thus become a significant factor in on-going ecumenical dialogue.[20] For our modest goal of understanding Matthew's portrayal of Peter, the notion of a developing Petrine tradition suggests that the apostle's role in the gospel is not reducible to that of representative disciple or mere "salvation-history primacy" but may indeed stand as a symbol and model of developing functions of pastoral leadership in Matthew's church.

In her study, *Peter: Apostle for the Whole Church*, another Roman

Catholic scholar, Pheme Perkins, agrees with many of the conclusions reached in *Peter in the New Testament* but is less confident about the presence of an evolving "trajectory" within the New Testament and early Christian writings.[21] Instead, she contends, the New Testament and other early writings witness to a plurality of traditions about Peter that may have certain overarching features but are not necessarily related in an evolving trajectory.

Matthew, she notes, emphasizes the role of Peter as a teacher who understands Jesus' teaching, in contrast to the "blind guides" that Jesus condemns (15:10-17; ch. 23). Even though Peter does not initially understand Jesus' teaching about what makes a person unclean, Jesus explains this "parable" to him (15:16-17). Two of the special Matthean texts on Peter (the question of defilement in 15:1-20 and the payment of the temple tax in 17:24-27) deal with issues that affected the relationships between Jews and Gentiles—issues important for Matthew's mixed community. In 18:21-35, Jesus instructs Peter on the lavish sense of forgiveness that is to characterize the community's discipline of errant members.

Despite the prominence given to Peter, however, he is not presented apart from the disciples, nor is he best understood as the "chief rabbi" of Matthew's community or as the "sole successor to Jesus" (p. 70). Instead, the figure of Peter serves in Matthew's gospel as the evangelist's way of assuring his community that the Christian practice of faithfully understanding and following Jesus' teachings will continue in the church both in its leadership and in the community as a whole.

After reviewing the rest of the New Testament and early Christian traditions on Peter, Perkins concludes that the apostle is consistently presented as a kind of bridge or mediating figure (as, for example, in Acts and Gal 1:18-24). He is not portrayed as the founder of any particular church but as an exemplary, if at times very human, disciple and as an apostolic founder of the early church as a whole. Within the diversity of New Testament traditions, Perkins observes, "no figure encompasses more of the diversity than Peter" (p. 184). This image of Peter provides a credible link to a renewed understanding of the Petrine office as a potential sign of unity among the diversity of contemporary Christian churches.

Matthew's Church and the Issue of Inclusion

If ecumenical concerns have driven studies of Matthew's portrayal of Peter and its implication for the nature of the church, feminist scholars have evaluated Matthew's portrayal of discipleship and church in relation to concerns about patriarchy and inclusion. At present, feminist studies of Matthew are relatively few; some scholars judge that such features as Matthew's emphasis on the male apostles, the frequent use of the address "Father" for God, and the more Jewish (and, in the mind of some, therefore more patriarchal) character of the gospel as a whole do not make it a promising venue. But other feminist scholars have challenged these assumptions by engaging in interesting and fruitful studies of the gospel.[22] As discussed above, the work of Amy-Jill Levine on Matthew's view of salvation history used a feminist perspective to underscore the gospel's inclusive and egalitarian perspectives.[23]

In her major study, *Towards a Feminist Critical Reading of the Gospel According to Matthew*, and in a recent commentary on the gospel, Elaine Mary Wainwright surveys the entire span of Matthew's narrative from a feminist perspective, with particular attention to Matthew's vision of discipleship and church.[24]

Her reading uncovers two seemingly contravailing tendencies in Matthew. On the one hand Matthew does have a strong patriarchal perspective: male characters have the authoritative roles and do the speaking; only men are listed as "disciples" and "apostles"; and the eleven apostles are entrusted with the on-going mission of Jesus at the conclusion of the gospel (28:16-20). Yet this androcentric perspective is punctuated by the substantial and exemplary role of women in the narrative, often in contrast to the weakness and infidelity of male disciples, from the women of the genealogy and Mary the mother of Jesus in the opening chapters to the significant place of women in the healing stories of chapters 8 and 9, the important mission role of the Canaanite woman in chapter 15, and the exemplary role of women at the climax of the gospel such as the woman who anoints Jesus (26:6-13), Pilate's wife who defends his innocence (27:19), and the women who stand by the cross (27:55-56), witness his burial and receive the message of the resurrection (27:61; 28:1-7, 8-10).

Wainwright believes that these two currents within the gospel reflect a struggle within Matthew's own community. More traditional patriarchal perspectives are countered by a vision of inclusion in which women are to participate in the community not on the basis of societal roles but as equal partners in the *basileia* proclaimed by Jesus (see, for example, 23:8-12). Wainwright suggests that although Matthew's community received a tradition (mediated through Mark's gospel) that identified "disciples" (*mathetai*) as a distinctively male group, the "placing of this tradition in the gospel context alongside stories of women's fidelity to Jesus and sayings of his regarding the inclusive nature of discipleship tended to modify its possibly exclusive character. For this reason it can be argued that the term *mathetai* functioned rhetorically and symbolically within the Matthean narrative as inclusive of all adherents to Jesus and the Jesus movement within the communities. Both women and men who had heard the message of Jesus, who understood it and now sought to live and teach it, constituted these communities."[25] Projecting such an inclusive vision of the community was, in fact, one of the fundamental purposes of Matthew's gospel, one reflected as well in his concern to open the community's horizon to Gentiles.[26]

In a study entitled "Gender Roles in a Scribal Community," Antoinette Wire noted the same conflicting currents within Matthew's gospel, using both feminist analysis and sociological models of community organization.[27] Drawing on studies of agrarian scribal communities in China under the Qing Dynasty (1644-1911), Wire detected five typical characteristics of such communities which she also finds evidence of in Pharisaic Judaism, Qumran and Matthew: "(1) They reinterpret in writing a revered literary tradition (2) in such a way as to teach concrete ritual and ethical behavior (3) which can assure the proper fulfillment of set roles within a community of identification (4) sanctioned by adequate rewards and punishments (5) in order to reassert right order in a situation where it is perceived to be under some threat" (p. 91).

The application of most of these criteria to Matthew's community as reflected in the gospel is not difficult. There is certainly in Matthew a concern for interpretation of revered tradition, both the Hebrew scriptures and Jesus' own teaching. Likewise Matthew's emphasis on practice and "doing the will of God" clearly attests to his ethical interest, and the important role of judgment in Matthew reflects a concern for sanctions. And most scholars agree that Matthew's community was in a time of acute transition.

The most difficult criterion to apply to Matthew, Wire concedes, is the third—namely, the assertion of right order within the community through determined roles. Here the apparently contravailing traditions already pointed out by Wainwright seem to disturb the model. While Matthew does emphasize the authoritative roles of the disciples and Peter within the world of the gospel, there is offsetting attention to the exemplary role of women and the "little ones." And in certain texts such as the strong critiques of 6:2, 5, 16; 21:28-32, most of the discourse in chapter 23, as well as the egalitarian vision of 23:8-10, Matthew seems intent on deflating or at least moderating traditional roles.

Wire attempts to explain this apparent contradiction in several ways. On one level, the lifting up of women and other minor characters in the gospel as exemplars of faith is meant as instruction to the disciples and helps reinforce their authoritative role. It is also possible that, unlike most scribal communities, there continued to be illiterate and economically deprived groups in the community, and the gospel wants the authoritative groups to be sensitive to this. Yet it may also be that this persistent egalitarian stream reflects a moderating influence of the Jesus tradition within the normal patterns of a scribal community. As Wire puts it, "the distinctive role of marginal people in this scribal community (i.e., Matthew's community) may be a vestige of the migration of the Jesus tradition from nonliterate and economically dependent culture into self-sufficient and classically educated culture. This vestige may be present not only in a literary sense but also in a social sense. Alongside this Gospel using marginal people's stories to instruct those the writer thinks bear responsibility for the tradition, very likely an oral tradition is operating in which people's voices still directly challenge others to faith" (pp. 120-121).

Undoubtedly, as feminist methodologies as well as those drawn from the social sciences continue to refine and expand their studies of the early community, more insight will be gained about Matthew's inclusive vision of the church.

Conclusion

Despite points of debate still unresolved and frustration in finding a comprehensive theological framework for Matthew's ecclesiology, the aspects of the gospel we have reviewed in this chapter truly confirm that

Notes

Preface

1. Cf. W.G. Kummel, *The New Testament: The History of the Investigation of Its Problems* (Nashville: Abingdon, 1972); Raymond F. Collins, *Introduction to the New Testament* (New York: Doubleday, 1983).

2. Cf. W. Marxsen, *Mark the Evangelist* (Nashville: Abingdon, 1969), a translation of a German work that first appeared in 1956; H. Conzelmann, *The Theology of Saint Luke* (London: Faber & Faber, 1960), first appearing in German in 1953; G. Bornkamm, G. Barth, H.J. Held, *Tradition and Interpretation in Matthew* (Philadelphia: Westminster, 1963); Bornkamm's essay, "The Stilling of the Storm in Matthew," included in this collection, had already appeared in German in 1948. On the entire method of redaction criticism, cf. N. Perrin, *What Is Redaction Criticism?* (Guides to Biblical Scholarship; Philadelphia: Fortress, 1969).

3. Cf. W.G. Thompson, *Matthew's Advice to a Divided Community*, Mt 17, 22–18, 35 (Analecta Biblica 44; Rome: Biblical Institute, 1970), 12-13, and especially "An Historical Perspective in the Gospel of Matthew," *Journal of Biblical Literature* 93 (1974) 244.

4. Cf. W.A. Beardslee, *Literary Criticism of the New Testament* (Guides to Biblical Scholarship; Philadelphia: Fortress, 1970) and the discussion in Mark Allan Powell, *What Is Narrative Criticism?* (Guides to Biblical Scholarship; Minneapolis: Augsburg Fortress, 1990) pp. 1-21.

5. On this point, see the comments of Graham Stanton in "The Communities of Matthew," *Interpretation* 46 (1992) 379-91 who notes that literary critics themselves are increasingly uncomfortable with a lack of interest in the social world that originally produced a text; see similar comments in Jack Dean Kingsbury, "Analysis of a Conversation" in David L. Balch (ed.), *Social History of the Matthean Community* (Minneapolis: Augsburg Fortress, 1991) pp. 259-63.

6. See the helpful discussion in Mark Allan Powell, *What Is Narrative Criticism?* pp. 11-44.

7. A helpful overview of studies of Matthew's gospel from 1945 to 1980 can be found in Graham Stanton, "The Origin and Purpose of Matthew's Gospel: Matthean Scholarship from 1945–1980," in *Aufstieg und Neidergang der Romanischer Welt* II. 25.3 (1985) 1889-1951 and his introduction to, G. Stanton (ed.), *The Interpretation of Matthew* (Edinburgh: T&T Clark, 2nd ed., 1995). A sampling of recent Matthean commentaries in English would include: W.D. Davies and Dale C. Allison, Jr., *Matthew* (International Critical Commentary; Edinburgh: T & T Clark, Vol. I (Matthew I-VII), 1988; Vol. II (Matthew VIII-XVIII), 1991; Richard B. Gardner, *Matthew* (Scottsdale: Herald Press, 1991); David E. Garland, *Reading Matthew: A Literary and Theological Commentary on the First Gospel* (New York: Crossroad, 1993); Douglas Hare, *Matthew* (Interpretation; Louisville: John Knox, 1993); Robert H. Smith, *Matthew* (Augsburg Commentary; Minneapolis: Augsburg, 1989); Robert H. Gundry, *Matthew: A Commentary on His Handbook for a Mixed Church Under Persecution* (Grand Rapids: Wm. B. Eerdmans, 2nd ed., 1994); Donald A. Hagner, *Matthew 1–13* (Word Biblical Commentary; Dallas: Word Publishing, 1993); Daniel J. Harrington, S.J., *The Gospel of Matthew* (Sacra Pagina; Collegeville: Liturgical Press, 1991); Ulrich Luz, *Matthew 1–7* (Minneapolis: Augsburg Fortress, 1989); John P. Meier, *Matthew* (New Testament Message 3; Collegeville: Liturgical Press, 1981); Leon Morris, *The Gospel According to Matthew* (Grand Rapids: Wm. B. Eerdmans, 1992); Augustine Stock, OSB, *The Method and Message of Matthew* (Collegeville: Liturgical Press, 1994); Benedict Viviano, O.P., "The Gospel According to Matthew," in Raymond Brown, S.S., Joseph Fitzmyer, S.J., Roland E. Murphy, O.Carm., *The New Jerome Biblical Commentary* (Englewood Cliffs: Prentice Hall, 1990).

8. Warren Carter, *What Are They Saying About Matthew's Sermon on the Mount?* (New York: Paulist, 1994).

1. The Setting for Matthew's Gospel

1. The term "Matthew's community" is used in a very generic sense. We do not know the size or complexity of the church to which Matthew's gospel was first directed. It may have consisted of several small household communities in a circumscribed local area. The reference to gathering the "ecclesia" or "church" to settle a dispute in 18:17 may suggest that the community was still fairly small but we cannot be sure.

2. For an evaluation of Papias' statement, cf. W.G. Kummel, *Introduction to the New Testament* (trans. by H.C. Kee; Nashville: Abingdon, rev. English ed., 1975) 120-21; and W.D. Davies and D. Allison, Jr., *Matthew*, Vol. I, 7-17.

3. W.D. Davies, *The Setting of the Sermon on the Mount* (Cambridge: Cambridge University, 1964); a briefer and more popular version of Davies' work is *The Sermon on the Mount* (Cambridge: Cambridge University, 1966). With some modification, Davies and Allison maintain this view in their recent commentary; see Vol. I, pp. 133-38.

4. On the role of the Pharisees, cf. J. Neusner, *From Politics to Piety: The Emergence of Pharisaic Judaism* (Englewood Cliffs: Prentice-Hall, 1973) and by the same author, *First Century Judaism in Crisis* (Nashville: Abingdon, 1975); also, Anthony J. Saldarini, *Pharisees, Scribes and Sadducees in Palestinian Society* (Wilmington: Michael Glazier, 1988). An account of the revolt and its aftermath through the writings of the first century historian Josephus is found in the work of D.M. Rhoads, *Israel in Revolution 6–74 C.E.* (Philadelphia: Fortress, 1976); see also Steve Mason, *Josephus and the New Testament* (Peabody: Hendrickson, 1992). For an overview of the Roman period, including the role of various factions, cf. Lester L. Grabbe, *Judaism from Cyrus to Hadrian* (Augsburg Fortress, 1992), Vol. 2: The Roman Period.

5. Quoted by Davies, *The Setting*, p. 275.

6. See the discussion in J. Andrew Overman, *Matthew's Gospel and Formative Judaism: The Social World of the Matthean Community* (Minneapolis: Augsburg Fortress, 1990), esp. pp. 38-43.

7. R. Hummel, *Die Auseinandersetzung zwischen Kirche und*

Judentum im Matthäusevangelium ("The Division between Church and Judaism in the Gospel of Matthew"; München: Kaiser Verlag, 1963).

8. Graham N. Stanton, *A Gospel for a New People: Studies in Matthew* (Edinburgh: T & T Clark, 1992); see also his article "The Communities of Matthew" in *Interpretation* 46 (1992) 379-391.

9. "The Communities of Matthew," pp. 385-86.

10. J. Andrew Overman, *Matthew's Gospel and Formative Judaism.*

11. The phrase "the true Israel" is never used by Matthew; yet this way of conceiving Matthew's perspective was already formulated by the late Wolfgang Trilling, *Das Wahre Israel* ("The True Israel"; STANT 10; München: Kösel-Verlag, 3rd rev. ed., 1964).

12. Anthony J. Saldarini, *Matthew's Christian-Jewish Community* (Chicago: University of Chicago, 1994).

13. D.R.A. Hare, *The Theme of Jewish Persecution of Christians in the Gospel According to St. Matthew* (Society for New Testament Studies Monograph Series 6; Cambridge: Cambridge University, 1967).

14. G. Strecker, *Der Weg der Gerechtigkeit: Untersuchung zur Theologie des Matthäus* (Göttingen: Vandenhoeck & Ruprecht, 2nd rev. ed., 1966).

15. David E. Garland, *The Intention of Matthew 23* (Novum Testamentum Sup. 52; Leiden: Brill, 1979); Sjef Van Tilborg, *The Jewish Leaders in Matthew* (Leiden: Brill, 1972).

16. Ulrich Luz, *Matthew 1-7: A Continental Commentary* (Minneapolis: Augsburg Fortress, 1989).

17. R. Hummel, *Die Auseinandersetzung.*

18. D. Hare, *The Theme of Jewish Persecution.*

19. Poul Nepper-Christensen, *Das Matthäusevangelium. Ein judenchristliches Evangelium?* ("The Gospel of Matthew. A Jewish Christian Gospel?" Aarhus: Universitetsforlaget, 1958).

20. J.P. Meier, *The Vision of Matthew: Christ, Church and Morality in the First Gospel* (Theological Inquiries: New York: Paulist, 1979).

21. J.D. Kingsbury, *Matthew* (Proclamation Commentaries: Philadelphia: Fortress, rev. ed., 1986); his views remain basically the same in his later work, *Matthew as Story* (Philadelphia: Fortress, rev. ed., 1988), pp. 147-60.

22. On the issue of the sources for Matthew's gospel, see the discussion in Chapter 2.

23. Raymond E. Brown and John P. Meier, *Antioch and Rome: New Testament Cradles of Christianity* (New York: Paulist, 1982).

24. Rodney Stark, "Antioch as the Social Situation for Matthew's Gospel," in D. Balch (ed.), *Social History of the Matthean Community*, pp. 189-210. A number of essays in this volume discuss the evidence for locating the Matthean community in Antioch or in the region of "upper Galilee" or "Syro-Phoenicia"; see, in particular, the dissenting voice of L. Michael White, "Crisis Management and Boundary Maintenance: The Social Location of the Matthean Community," who argues that the evidence of the social milieu detectable in Matthew's gospel is not persuasive for an urban location such as Antioch but that a Galilean location under the reign of Herod Agrippa II is more probable (pp. 211-47).

25. See the evaluation of possible locations in J. Meier, *Antioch and Rome*, pp. 18-27.

26. B.T. Viviano, "Where Was the Gospel According to Matthew Written?" *Catholic Biblical Quarterly* 41 (1979) 533-46.

27. J. Andrew Overman, *Matthew's Gospel and Formative Judaism*, pp. 158-59.

28. Jack Dean Kingsbury, *Matthew*, pp. 105-07; see the thorough evaluations of Papias' statement and speculation about the author of Matthew in W. D. Davies and Dale Allison, Jr., *Matthew*, Volume I, pp. 7-58; also Ulrich Luz, *Matthew 1-7*, pp. 93-95.

29. See below, Chapter 2.

30. On this see D. Senior, "The Ministry of Continuity: Matthew's Gospel and the Interpretation of History," *The Bible Today* 82 (1976) 670-76 and "The Gospel of Matthew and Our Jewish Heritage," *The Bible Today* 27 (1989) 325-32.

31. Anthony J. Saldarini, *Matthew's Christian-Jewish Community*, p. 113.

2. The Sources and Structure of the Gospel

1. For a thorough discussion, see Frans Neirynck, "Synoptic Problem," in R. Brown, S.S., J. Fitzmyer, S.J., and R. Murphy, O.Carm., *The New Jerome Biblical Commentary*, pp. 587-95.

2. G. Bornkamm, "The Authority to 'Bind' and 'Loose' in the Church

in Matthew's Gospel: The Problem of Sources in Matthew's Gospel," in *Jesus and Man's Hope* (Pittsburgh: Pittsburgh Theological Seminary, 1970), Volume 1, pp. 37-50.

3. D. Senior, *The Passion Narrative According to Matthew: A Redactional Study* (Bibliotheca Ephemeridum Theologicarum Lovaniensium 39; Louvain: Louvain University, 1975); a more popular version of this study is D. Senior, *The Passion of Jesus in the Gospel of Matthew* (Passion Series 1; Collegeville: Liturgical Press, 1985).

4. B.C. Butler, *The Originality of St. Matthew: A Critique of the Two-Document Hypothesis* (Cambridge: Cambridge University, 1951).

5. William R. Farmer, *The Synoptic Problem: A Critical Analysis* (Dillsboro: Western North Carolina Press, 1976, a reprint of the 1964 edition, New York: Macmillan). In a more recent work, Farmer intensifies his arguments against the two-source hypothesis by suggesting that it undermines the authority of the canonical gospels by introducing the prospect of an older and alternate portrayal of Jesus in the guise of "Q" which purports not to include any reference to the passion of Jesus; see William R. Farmer, *The Gospel of Jesus* (Louisville: Westminster John Knox, 1994).

6. M.D. Goulder, *Midrash and Lection in Matthew* (London: SPCK, 1974).

7. W.F. Albright and C.S. Mann, *Matthew* (The Anchor Bible 26; Garden City: Doubleday, 1971).

8. This is true, for example, of recent commentaries such as those by W.D. Davies and D. Allison, D. Garland, D. Hare, D. Harrington, U. Luz, and J. Meier (for titles, see note 7 in the Preface).

9. Cf. a thorough discussion of the issue in F. Neirynck, *Minor Agreements of Matthew and Luke Against Mark, with a Consultative List* (Bibliotheca Ephemeridum Theologicarum Lovaniensium 37; Louvain: Louvain University, 1974), and his more recent contribution, "The Minor Agreements and Q," in Ronald A. Piper (ed.), *The Gospel Behind the Gospels: Current Studies on Q* (Supplements to Novum Testamentum 75; Leiden: Brill, 1995), pp. 49-72.

10. W.G. Thompson, *Matthew's Advice to a Divided Community. Mt. 17, 22–18,35* (Analecta Biblica 44; Rome: Biblical Institute, 1970).

11. David R. Bauer, *The Structure of Matthew's Gospel: A Study in Literary Design* (JSNTS 31; Sheffield: The Almond Press, 1989).

12. B.W. Bacon, *Studies in Matthew* (London: Constable, 1930), and by the same author, "The 'Five Books' of Matthew against the Jews," *The Expositor* 15 (1918) 55-66.

13. However, Dale C. Allison, Jr., has recently argued for the fundamental importance of Moses typology in Matthew; see his study, *The New Moses: A Matthean Typology* (Minneapolis: Augsburg Fortress, 1993) and the comments below in Chapter 6.

14. H. Frankemölle, *Jahwebund und Kirche Christi* (Neutestamentliche Abhandlungen 10; Münster: Aschendorff, 1974).

15. Dale C. Allison, Jr., "Matthew: Structure, Biographical Impulse and the *Imitatio Christi*," in F. Van Segbroeck et al. (eds.), *The Four Gospels*, Vol. II, 1203-21.

16. P.F. Ellis, *Matthew: His Mind and His Message* (Collegeville: The Liturgical Press, 1974).

17. For a fuller description of the chiastic structure Ellis perceives in Matthew, see ibid., p. 12.

18. John Paul Heil, *The Death and Resurrection of Jesus: A Narrative-Critical Reading of Matthew 26–28* (Minneapolis: Augsburg Fortress, 1991) and his earlier article, "The Narrative Structure of Matthew 27:55–28:20," *Journal of Biblical Literature* 110 (1991) 419-38.

19. For further discussion of Heil's proposed structure, with particular implications for Matthew's passion narrative, see D. Senior, "Matthew's Account of the Burial of Jesus Mt 27,57-61," in F. Van Segbroeck, C.M. Tuckett, G. Van Belle, J. Verheyden (eds.), *The Four Gospels 1992: Festschrift Frans Neirynck* (Leuven: University Press, 1992) 1433-48.

20. U. Luz, *Matthew 1-7*, p. 38.

21. J.D. Kingsbury, *Matthew: Structure, Christology, Kingdom* (Philadelphia: Fortress, 1975); E. Krentz, "The Extent of Matthew's Prologue: Toward the Structure of the First Gospel," *Journal of Biblical Literature* 83 (1964) 409-15.

22. J.D. Kingsbury, *Matthew as Story* (Philadelphia: Fortress, 2nd rev. ed., 1988).

23. His formulations of the overall themes of each major section is: "The presentation of Jesus" (1:1–4:16); "The ministry of Jesus to Israel and Israel's repudiation of Jesus" (4:17–16:20); "The journey of Jesus

to Jerusalem and his suffering, death and resurrection" (16:21-28:20). See *Matthew as Story*.

24. As D.C. Allison observes, this tripartite division after all may simply tell us that Matthew's gospel, like most stories, has "a beginning, a middle, and an end"; see "Matthew: Structure, Biographical Impulse and the *Imitatio Christi*," in F. Van Segbroeck et al. (eds.), *The Four Gospels*, Vol. II, 1203.

25. Frans Neirynck, "*Apo Tote Erkzato* and the Structure of Matthew," in F. Van Segbroeck (ed.), *Evangelica II 1982-1991.* Collected Essays by Frans Neirynck (Leuven: University Press, 1991) 141-82. This article first appeared in *Ephemerides Theologicae Lovanienses* 64 (1988) 21-59.

26. See the discussion of Peter in Matthew in Chapter 7.

27. J.D. Kingsbury, *Matthew: Structure*, p. 8; D. Bauer, *The Structure of Matthew's Gospel*, p. 44.

28. On this point, see D. Senior, *The Passion Narrative*, 47-50.

29. Neirynck provides a simple schematic picture of what he means (see "The Structure of Matthew," p. 178): Mt 4:12-17 6:13-2326-28

30. D. Bauer, *The Structure of Matthew's Gospel*, 13-20.

31. Frank Matera has suggested that the evangelist works around certain key events or "kernels" in the story of Jesus' life, building his overall plot in this manner as it moves inexorably from Jesus' offer of salvation, its rejection by Israel and its subsequent offer to the Gentiles at the end of the gospel; see. F. Matera, "The Plot of Matthew's Gospel," *Catholic Biblical Quarterly* 49 (1987) 233-53. Mark Alan Powell, however, finds the contributions of Kingsbury and Matera useful but incomplete. As Kingsbury emphasizes, the key verses of 4:17 and 16:21 sound fundamental themes of proclamation (4:17) and rejection (16:21) that carry Matthew's story toward its resolution. The main plot is one announced in 1:21: Jesus will save God's people from their sins despite the efforts of Satan to thwart God's plan. This is the fundamental coherence that will carry the story through (as Matera suggests). But there are also important subplots, one involving the religious leaders and the mystery of Israel's rejection of Jesus, and the other the disciples whose failure to fully comprehend or adequately respond to Jesus is also an obstacle. Only in taking into account both underlying plot and key subplots does the full span of Matthew's story become apparent; see M.

Powell, "The Plot and Subplots of Matthew's Gospel," *New Testament Studies* 38 (1992) 187-204.

32. See the more detailed discussion in D. Senior, "Matthew's Account of the Burial of Jesus Mt 27,57-61," in F. Van Segbroeck et al. (eds.), *The Four Gospels*, 1433-48, esp. pp. 1441-42.

3. Matthew's View of Salvation History

1. On Matthew's use of the Old Testament, see below, Chapter 4.

2. John P. Meier, *The Vision of Matthew*, p. 30.

3. Cf. the discussion of Matthew's milieu in Chapter 1.

4. Rolf Walker, *Die Heilsgeschichte im ersten Evangelium* (Göttingen: Vandenhoeck & Ruprecht, 1967).

5. G. Strecker, "Das Geschichtsverstandnis des Matthäus," *Evangelische Theologie* 26 (1966) 57-74; an English translation appeared in the *Journal of the American Academy of Religion* 35 (1967) 219-30.

6. See the discussion about the role of these verses in the structure of Matthew, above, Chapter 2.

7. J. Meier, "Salvation History in Matthew: In Search of a Starting Point," *Catholic Biblical Quarterly* 37 (1975) 203-15; *Law and History in Matthew's Gospel: A Redactional Study of Mt. 5:17-48* (Analecta Biblica 71; Rome: Biblical Institute, 1976); *The Vision of Matthew* (1979).

8. J. Meier, *The Vision of Matthew*, p. 34.

9. For a discussion of this passage and its background in the Old Testament and Judaism, cf. D. Senior, "The Death of Jesus and the Resurrection of the Holy Ones (Mt 27:51-53)," *Catholic Biblical Quarterly* 38 (1976) 312-29; also in *The Passion of Jesus in the Gospel of Matthew* (Passion Series 1; Collegeville: Liturgical Press, 1985) 141-48.

10. J. Meier, *The Vision of Matthew*, p. 37.

11. On Matthew's attitude to the Jewish law, see below, Chapter 4.

12. J.D. Kingsbury, *Matthew: Structure, Christology, Kingdom*, pp. 1-39.

13. Ibid., p. 31.

14. Ibid.

15. David B. Howell, *Matthew's Inclusive Story. A Study in the*

Narrative Rhetoric of the First Gospel (JSNTS 42; Sheffield: Sheffield Academic Press, 1990).

16. Amy-Jill Levine, *The Social and Ethnic Dimensions of Matthean Salvation History. "Go nowhere among the Gentiles..." (Matt. 10:5b)* (Studies in the Bible and Early Christianity 14; Lewiston: The Edwin Mellon Press, 1988).

17. A. Levine, *The Social and Ethnic Dimensions*, p. 274.

4. Matthew's Use of the Old Testament

1. On the best characterization of these special Old Testament quotations in Matthew, cf. W.G. Kummel, *Introduction to the New Testament*, p. 110, n. 23. He argues that the term "fulfillment quotations" coined by Rothfuchs is preferable since it points to the function of the quotations. The term "formula quotations" has been used by scholars since the turn of the century. Some interpreters exclude 2:6 from the list because it does not have the term "fulfill" in the introductory formula, and 26:56 because it speaks of the "scriptures of the prophets" being fulfilled but does not cite any specific text. This verse from Matthew's passion narrative is similar to Mark 14:49 ("but let the scriptures be fulfilled"); its application of the Old Testament to the events of the passion may have been an important starting point for Matthew's use of Old Testament fulfillment texts in application to other events of Jesus' life. On this cf. D. Senior, *The Passion Narrative*, 151-55.

2. K. Stendahl, *The School of St. Matthew and Its Use of the Old Testament* (Philadelphia: Fortress, first American ed., 1968).

3. Stendahl detects strict rules or guidelines that the Qumran community used in this type of scriptural interpretation; *The School of St. Matthew*, pp. 191-92.

4. Ibid., p. vi.

5. See the comments of G. Stanton, *A Gospel for a New People*, p. 350; and U. Luz, *Matthew 1-7*, p. 160.

6. R.H. Gundry, *The Use of the Old Testament in St. Matthew's Gospel with Special Reference to the Messianic Hope* (Supplements to *Novum Testamentum* 18; Leiden: E.J. Brill, 1967).

7. Gundry elaborates on his reasons for the early dating of Matthew in his commentary, *Matthew: A Commentary on His Literary and*

Theological Art (Grand Rapids: William B. Eerdmans, 2nd ed., 1994), pp. 599-622.

8. W. Rothfuchs, *Die Erfüllungszitate des Matthäus-Evangeliums: Eine biblisch-theologische Untersuchung* (Beitrage zur Wissenschaft vom Alten und Neuen Testament 8; Stuttgart: W. Kohlhammer, 1969).

9. Cf. the discussion of Strecker's viewpoint, above, Chapter 3.

10. Cf. J.D. Kingsbury, *The Parables of Jesus in Matthew 13: A Study in Redaction Criticism* (Richmond: John Knox, 1969), pp. 12-15; for a different approach to the entire parable discourse, cf. J. Dupont, "Le point de vue de Matthieu dans le chapitre des paraboles," in *L'Évangile selon Matthieu: Rédaction et Théologie* (ed. M. Didier; Bibliotheca Ephemeridum Theologicarum Lovaniensium 29; Gembloux: Duculot, 1972), pp. 221-60.

11. This is similar to the view of G.D. Kilpatrick, *The Origins of the Gospel According to St. Matthew* (Oxford: Clarendon, 1946).

12. F. Van Segbroeck, "Les citations d'accomplissement dans l'Évangile selon Matthieu d'après trois ouvrages récents," in *L'Évangile selon Matthieu* (ed. M. Didier), pp. 107-30.

13. A proponent of earlier dating for the gospels and most of the New Testament books is J.A.T. Robinson in his work, *Redating the New Testament* (Philadelphia: Westminster, 1976). He claims that there is no evidence in the gospels that the evangelists were aware of the destruction of Jerusalem, and that therefore all of them were written prior to A.D. 70.

14. G. Stanton, *A Gospel for a New People*, p. 355.

15. Ibid., p. 358.

16. R. Brown, *The Birth of the Messiah* (Garden City: Doubleday, 1977), pp. 98-99, suggests that in contrast to the passion of Jesus the application of scriptural fulfillment to the events of Jesus' origin may have been relatively undeveloped in early Christian preaching. Thus Matthew gave his attention to this relatively "unexplored" territory; see also, G. Stanton, *A Gospel for a New People*, p. 360.

17. D. Howell, *Matthew's Inclusive Story*, pp. 185-90.

18. U. Luz, *Matthew 1-7*, p. 162; similarly, R. Brown: "For Matthew, these citations did more than highlight incidental agreements between the OT and Jesus. He introduced them because they fit his general

theology of the oneness of God's plan...." *The Birth of the Messiah*, p. 104.

19. U. Luz, *Matthew 1-7*, p. 157.

5. Matthew's Attitude to the Law

1. In relationship to the sermon on the mount, especially Mt 5:17-18, see W. Carter, *What Are They Saying About Matthew's Sermon on the Mount?* pp. 84-88.

2. On this see the observations of U. Luz, *Matthew 1-7*, pp. 270-73.

3. This is true, for example, of the studies of R. Hammerton-Kelly, K. Snodgrass (cf. below) and J. Meier, *The Vision of Matthew*. On the whole issue of the Jewish law and Christianity, see the thoughtful essay of W.D. Davies, "The Significance of the Law in Christianity," in *Christians and Jews* (eds. H. Küng and W. Kasper; Concilium; New York: Seabury, 1974), 24-32.

4. Many scholars agree that in these instances, the Matthean Jesus has radicalized the law to the point of contravening it; on this cf. J. Meier, *Law and History in Matthew's Gospel*, pp. 140-61.

5. G. Barth, "Matthew's Understanding of the Law," in *Tradition and Interpretation in Matthew* (Philadelphia: Westminster, 1963), 58-164.

6. This position is similar to that of R. Hummel, discussed above in Chapter 1.

7. Cf. E. Schweizer, "Observance of the Law and Charismatic Activity in Matthew," *New Testament Studies* 16 (1970) 213-30; but see D. Hill, "False Prophets and Charismatics: Structure and Interpretation in Matthew 7.15-23," *Biblica* 57 (1976) 327-48 who contends that the charismatics Matthew disputes are not likely to have been anti-law. The term *anomia* in Matthew may simply mean those who disobey the will of God.

8. Hans Dieter Betz, *Essays on the Sermon on the Mount* (Philadelphia: Fortress, 1985); and "The Sermon on the Mount in Matthew's Interpretation," in B.A. Pearson (ed.), *The Future of Early Christianity: Essays in Honor of Helmut Koester* (Minneapolis: Fortress, 1991) 258-75.

9. G. Stanton provides a detailed critique of Betz's interpretation in

A Gospel for a New People, 307-25. The sermon is integral to the narrative framework of Matthew and its ethical demands are based on a strong Christology.

10. R.G. Hammerton-Kelly, "Attitudes to the Law in Matthew's Gospel: a Discussion of Matthew 5:18," *Biblical Research* 17 (1972) 19-32.

11. Robert Guelich, *The Sermon on the Mount: A Foundation for Understanding* (Dallas: Word Publishing, 1982).

12. See, for example, the works of A. Sand and J. Meier, discussed below.

13. R. Banks, "Matthew's Understanding of the Law: Authenticity and Interpretation in Matthew 5:17-20," *Journal of Biblical Literature* 93 (1974) 243-62; see also by the same author, *Jesus and the Law in the Synoptic Tradition* (Society for New Testament Studies Monograph Series 28; Cambridge: Cambridge University, 1975). In his book, Banks concentrates on the question of Jesus' own attitude to the law rather than the theology of Matthew.

14. R. Banks, "Matthew's Understanding of the Law," pp. 229-32.

15. See above, Chapter 3.

16. J. Meier, *The Vision of Matthew*, p. 262.

17. A. Sand, *Das Gesetz und die Propheten: Untersuchungen zur Theologie des Evangeliums nach Matthäus* (Biblische Untersuchungen 11; Regensburg: Friedrich Pustet, 1974); see also his later commentary on the gospel, *Das Evangelium nach Matthäus* (Regensburg: Friedrich Pustet, 1986).

18. On the background and use of this key term in Matthew, cf. B. Przybylski, *Righteousness in Matthew and His World of Thought* (Society for New Testament Studies Monograph Series 41; Cambridge: Cambridge University, 1980).

19. Klyne R. Snodgrass, "Matthew's Understanding of the Law," *Interpretation* 46 (1992) 368-78.

20. Dale C. Allison, Jr., *The New Moses: A Matthean Typology* (Minneapolis: Augsburg Fortress, 1993); W.D. Davies & Dale C. Allison, Jr., *Matthew*. Volume I: Introduction and Commentary on Matthew I-VII (International Critical Commentary; Edinburgh: T & T Clark, 1988).

21. U. Luz, *Matthew 1-7*.

22. U. Luz, *Matthew 1-7*, p. 163. It is noteworthy that A. Saldarini, in considering the same material, comes to a similar conclusion; namely that Matthew is presenting the "torah of Jesus" (see *Matthew's Christian-Jewish Community*, pp. 124-64; Saldarini's general interpretation of Matthew was taken up in Chapter 1). But unlike Luz, Saldarini finds this as support for his thesis that Matthew still operated within the orbit of Judaism, albeit as a deviant community. It is striking, however, that Luz gives much more attention to Christology than Saldarini; in his chapter on Matthew's view of the law, Saldarini surveys the various positions the Matthean Jesus assumes about the law but gives only minimal attention to 5:17-20 and less to the narrative force of the gospel as a whole.

6. Matthew's Christology

1. On this see Raymond E. Brown, *An Introduction to New Testament Christology* (New York: Paulist, 1994); James D.G. Dunn, *Christology in the Making* (Philadelphia: Westminster, 1980); Walter Kasper, *Jesus the Christ* (New York: Paulist, 1976); and Pheme Perkins and Reginald Fuller, *Who Is This Christ?* (Philadelphia: Fortress, 1983).

2. J.D. Kingsbury, *Matthew: Structure, Christology, Kingdom* (Philadelphia: Fortress, 1975), esp. pp. 40-127; *Jesus Christ in Matthew, Mark, and Luke* (Proclamation Commentaries; Philadelphia: Fortress, 1981), pp. 64-73; *Matthew as Story* (Philadelphia: Fortress, 2nd rev. ed., 1988).

3. On Davidic motifs in Matthew, particularly in the infancy narrative, cf. B.M. Nolan, *The Royal Son of God: The Christology of Matthew 1-2 in the Setting of the Gospel* (Orbis Biblicus et Orientalis 23; Göttingen: Vandenhoeck & Ruprecht, 1979).

4. J.D. Kingsbury, *Matthew: Structure, Christology, Kingdom*, p. 121.

5. J.D. Kingsbury, *Matthew as Story*, pp. 95-103.

6. J.D. Kingsbury, *Matthew: Structure, Christology, Kingdom*, pp. 121-22.

7. See, for example, G. Strecker, *Der Weg der Gerechtigkeit*, pp. 123-26, and W. Trilling, *Das Wahre Israel: Studien zur Theologie des Matthäus Evangeliums* (München: Kosel, 3rd ed., 1964), pp. 21-51.

8. J.D. Kingsbury, *Matthew: Structure, Christology, Kingdom*, p. 106.

9. Donald Verseput, for example, agrees that Son of God is the key title for Matthew's Christology but faults Kingsbury for seeing other titles as somehow "subordinate" to it or in tension with it. Jesus' identity as Son of God is presented by Matthew without elaboration or polemic. This title, Verseput maintains, was strongly Christian in character and the unique relationship between Jesus and God implied in this title informs the messianic identity of Jesus expressed in other titles such as Son of David or Christ. See D. Verseput, "The Role and Meaning of the 'Son of God' Title in Matthew's Gospel," *New Testament Studies* 33 (1987) 532-56; also, the comments of G. Stanton, *A Gospel for a New People*, p. 170, who emphasizes the unique role of the Son of David title in Matthew.

10. David Hill, "Son and Servant: An Essay on Matthean Christology," *Journal for the Study of the New Testament* 6 (1980) 2-16. Hill and Kingsbury have publicly exchanged views on this issue: see D. Hill, "The Figure of Jesus in Matthew's Gospel: A Response to Professor Kingsbury's Literary-Critical Probe," *Journal for the Study of the New Testament* 21 (1984) 37-52; and Kingsbury's response, "The Figure of Jesus in Matthew's Story: A Rejoinder to David Hill," *Journal for the Study of the New Testament* 25 (1985) 61-81.

11. On the role of Isaiah 42:1-4 in this passage, see the study of L. Cope, *Matthew: A Scribe Trained for the Kingdom of Heaven* (The Catholic Biblical Quarterly Monograph Series 5; Washington: Catholic Biblical Association of America, 1976), pp. 32-51.

12. Cf. B. Gerhardsson, *The Mighty Acts of Jesus According to Matthew* (Lund: CWK Gleerup, 1979), esp. pp. 88-91.

13. John Meier, *The Vision of Matthew*, pp. 210-19; on the background and use of the Son of Man title in Matthew as well as in other New Testament texts, see Douglas R. A. Hare, *The Son of Man Tradition* (Minneapolis: Fortress, 1990).

14. G. Stanton, *A Gospel for a New People*, pp. 169-91.

15. See Mt 1:1; 9:27; 12:23; 15:22; 20:30,31 (here Mt is parallel to Mk 10:47,48); 21:9, 15; 22:42 (see Mk 12:35).

16. Bruce J. Malina and Jerome H. Neyrey, *Calling Jesus Names: The Social Value of Labels in Matthew* (Sonoma, CA: Polebridge Press, 1988).

17. Dale C. Allison, Jr., *The New Moses: A Matthean Typology* (Minneapolis: Fortress, 1993).

18. M.J. Suggs, *Wisdom, Christology, and Law in Matthew's Gospel* (Cambridge: Harvard University, 1970).

19. On this see, James Dunn, *Christology in the Making*, pp. 163-212.

20. M.D. Johnson, "Reflections on a Wisdom Approach to Matthew's Christology," *Catholic Biblical Quarterly* 36 (1974) 44-64.

21. F.W. Burnett, *The Testament of Jesus-Sophia: A Redaction-Critical Study of the Eschatological Discourse in Matthew* (Washington: University Press of America, 1981).

22. C. Deutsch, "Wisdom in Matthew: Transformation of a Symbol," *Novum Testamentum* 32 (1990) 13-47, as well as her earlier dissertation, a study of Mt 25:30, *Hidden Wisdom and the Easy Yoke: Wisdom, Torah and Disciples in Matthew* 11:25,30 (JSNT SS18; Sheffield: University of Sheffield Press, 1987).

23. See, for example, R. Brown, *The Gospel According to John I-XII* (The Anchor Bible 29; Garden City: Doubleday, 1966), pp. cxxii-cxxv; and J. Dunn, *Christology in the Making*.

24. See the assessment of W.D. Davies and D. Allison in *The Gospel According to Matthew*, Vol. 2, p. 295.

25. H.J. Held, "Matthew as Interpreter of the Miracle Stories," in *Tradition and Interpretation in Matthew*, pp. 165-299.

26. See, for example, W.G. Thompson, "Reflections on the Composition of Mt. 8:1-9:34," *Catholic Biblical Quarterly* 33 (1971) 365-88, and J.P. Heil, "Significant Aspects of the Healing Miracles in Matthew," *Catholic Biblical Quarterly* 41 (1979) 274-87.

27. J.D. Kingsbury, "Observations on the 'Miracle Chapters' of Matthew 8-9," *Catholic Biblical Quarterly* 40 (1978) 559-73.

28. C. Burger, "Jesu Täten nach Matthäus 8 und 9," *Zeitschrift für Theologie und Kirche* 70 (1973) 272-73.

29. J. D. Kingsbury, "Observations on the Miracle Chapters," pp. 572-73.

30. J. D. Kingsbury, *Matthew as Story*, p. 69.

31. B. Gerhardsson, *The Mighty Acts of Jesus According to Matthew*.

32. On this see, D. Senior, "The Jesus of Matthew," *Church* 5 (1989) 10-13.

33. On the exemplary role of Matthew's portrayal of Jesus, see Charles E. Carlston, "Christology and Church in Matthew," in F. Van Segbroeck et al., *The Four Gospels*, vol. 2, 1283-1304 and D. Howell, *Matthew's Inclusive Story*, 251-59.

34. R.T. France, *Matthew: Evangelist and Teacher* (Grand Rapids: Zondervan, 1989), 278-317.

7. *Matthew's View of Discipleship and Church*

1. H. Frankemölle, *Jahwebund und Kirche Christi*. Studien zur Form- und Traditionsgeschichte des "Evangeliums" nach Matthäus (Neutestamentliche Abhandlungen 10; Münster, 1974).

2. For a broader discussion of the form and possible Old Testament background of Matthew 28:16-20, cf. B.J. Hubbard, *The Matthean Redaction of a Primitive Apostolic Commissioning: An Exegesis of Matthew 28:16-20* (SBL Dissertation Series 19; Missoula: Society of Biblical Literature, 1974).

3. Cf. J.D. Kingsbury's critique of Frankemölle on this point in *Matthew: Structure, Christology, Kingdom*, pp. 37-39.

4. On the role of the disciples in Matthew, see in addition to the authors treated below, G. Barth, *Tradition and Interpretation in Matthew*, pp. 105-24; U. Luz, "Die Jünger im Matthäusevangelium," *Zeitschrift für Neuentestamentliche Wissenschaft* 62 (1971) 141-71; M. Sheridan, "Disciples and Discipleship in Matthew and Luke," *Biblical Theology Bulletin* 3 (1973) 235-55; Richard A. Edwards, "Uncertain Faith: Matthew's Portrait of the Disciples," in F. Segovia (ed.), *Discipleship in the New Testament* (Philadelphia: Fortress, 1985), pp. 47-61.

5. J. Zumstein, *La Condition du Croyant dans L'Évangile selon Matthieu* (Orbis Biblicus et Orientalis 16; Göttingen: Vandenhoeck & Ruprecht, 1977).

6. On this, see P. Minear, "The Disciples and Crowds in the Gospel of Matthew," *Anglican Theological Review* Supplementary Series 3 (1974) 28.

7. On the symbolic role of Jesus' opponents in Matthew, see S. Van Tilborg, *The Jewish Leaders in Matthew* (Leiden: E.J.Brill, 1972); D.E. Garland, *The Intention of Matthew 23*.

8. See, below, the work of David E. Orton on the role of the "scribe" in Matthew's gospel.

9. On the community discourse of Matthew 18 as an important source for his ecclesiology, cf. W.G. Thompson, *Matthew's Advice to a Divided Community*, and W. Pesch, *Matthäus der Seelsorger: Das neue Verständnis der Evangelien dargestellet am Beispiel von Matthäus 18* (Stuttgarter BibelStudien 2; Stuttgart: Katholisches Bibelwerk, 1966).

10. David E. Orton, *The Understanding Scribe: Matthew and the Apocalyptic Ideal* (JSNT SS25; Sheffield: University of Sheffield Press, 1989).

11. D. Orton, *The Understanding Scribe*, pp. 161-62.

12. Michael H. Crosby, *House of Disciples: Church, Economics & Justice in Matthew* (Maryknoll, NY: Orbis, 1988).

13. J.D. Kingsbury, "The Figure of Peter in Matthew's Gospel as a Theological Problem," *Journal of Biblical Literature* 98 (1979) 67-83.

14. Ibid., pp. 72-74.

15. Michael J. Wilkins, *The Concept of Disciple in Matthew's Gospel: As Reflected in the Use of the Term Mathetes* (Supplements to Novum Testamentum 59; Leiden: E.J. Brill, 1988).

16. Arlo J. Nau, *Peter in Matthew: Discipleship, Diplomacy, and Dispraise* (Good News Studies 36; Collegeville, MN: Liturgical Press, 1992).

17. R. Brown, K. Donfried, J. Reumann (eds.), *Peter in the New Testament: A Collaborative Assessment by Protestant and Roman Catholic Scholars* (Minneapolis: Augsburg/New York: Paulist, 1973).

18. R. Brown, *Biblical Reflections on Crises Facing the Church* (New York: Paulist, 1975), pp. 63-83.

19. *Peter in the New Testament*, pp. 162-68.

20. R. Brown, *Biblical Reflections*, p. 77.

21. Pheme Perkins, *Peter: Apostle for the Whole Church* (Columbia: University of South Carolina Press, 1994), esp. pp. 66-80.

22. See, for example, Janice Capel Anderson, "Matthew: Gender and Reading," *Semeia* 28 (1983) 3-27; Jane Kopas, "Jesus and Women in Matthew," *Theology Today* 47 (1990) 13-21; Jane Schaberg offered a feminist interpretation of the infancy narratives of Matthew and Luke in *The Illegitimacy of Jesus* (San Francisco: Harper & Row, 1987).

23. See above, Chapter 3.

24. Elaine Mary Wainwright, *Towards a Feminist Critical Reading of The Gospel According to Matthew* (BZNT 60; Berlin/New York: Walter de Gruyter, 1991); and "The Gospel of Matthew," in Elisabeth Schüssler Fiorenza (ed.), *Search the Scriptures: A Feminist Commentary*. Volume 2 (New York: Crossroad, 1994), pp. 635-77.

25. E. Wainwright, *Towards a Feminist Critical Reading*, p. 335. David Howell makes a similar point in his consideration of the disciples in Matthew. In addition to the explicitly designated "disciples" the gospel narrative uses many other characters, including "minor" ones, to exemplify authentic discipleship. Even the opponents of Jesus through their negative example contribute to an understanding of what true discipleshp means; see D. Howell, *Matthew's Inclusive Story*, pp. 233-36.

26. "This paradigm (of inclusion) seems to encode a vision that had been kept alive by the community itself, but its preservation within this final stage of redaction and its skillful incorporation into the text would also function to challenge other paradigms of discipleship and of participation in the fruits of the kingdom that were present in the community and were likewise encoded in the Gospel. This explains a tension that has not been avoided but is in fact at the heart of the stated purpose in redacting—to bring out the new and the old." *The Gospel of Matthew*, p. 676.

27. Antoinette Clark Wire, "Gender Roles in a Scribal Community," in D. Balch (ed.), *Social History of the Matthean Community*, pp. 87-121.

Select Bibliography

(This bibliography is restricted to works on Matthew
cited in this study.)

Albright, W.F. and C.S. Mann. *Matthew*. The Anchor Bible 26. Garden City: Doubleday, 1971.

Allison, Jr., Dale C. "Matthew: Structure, Biographical Impulse and the *Imitatio Christi*." In *The Four Gospels 1992: Festschrift Frans Neirynck*, ed. F. Van Segbroeck, C.M. Tuckett, G. Van Belle, and J. Verheyden, 1203-21. Volume II. Leuven: University Press, 1992.

_____. *The New Moses: A Matthean Typology*. Minneapolis: Augsburg Fortress, 1993.

Anderson, Janice Capel. "Matthew: Gender and Reading." *Semeia* 28 (1983): 3-27.

Bacon, B.W. "The Five Books of Matthew against the Jews." *The Expositor* 15 (1918): 55-66.

_____. *Studies in Matthew*. London: Constable, 1930.

Banks, R. "Matthew's Understanding of the Law: Authenticity and Interpretation in Matthew 5:17-20." *Journal of Biblical Literature* 93 (1974): 243-62.

_____. *Jesus and the Law in the Synoptic Tradition.* Society for New Testament Studies Monograph Series 28. Cambridge: Cambridge University, 1975.

Barth, G. *Tradition and Interpretation in Matthew.* Philadelphia: Westminster, 1963.

Bauer, David R. *The Structure of Matthew's Gospel: A Study in Literary Design.* JSNTS 31. Sheffield: The Almond Press, 1989.

Betz, Hans Dieter. *Essays on the Sermon on the Mount.* Philadelphia: Fortress, 1985.

_____. "The Sermon on the Mount in Matthew's Interpretation." In *The Future of Early Christianity: Essays in Honor of Helmut Koester*, ed. B.A. Pearson. Minneapolis: Fortress, 1991, 258-75.

Bornkamm, G. "The Authority to Bind and Loose in the Church in Matthew's Gospel: The Problem of Sources in Matthew's Gospel." In *Jesus and Man's Hope.* Volume 1. Pittsburgh: Pittsburgh Theological Seminary, 1970, 37-50.

Bornkamm, G., G. Barth, and H.J. Held. *Tradition and Interpretation in Matthew.* Philadelphia: Westminster, 1963.

Brown, Raymond E. *Biblical Reflections on Crises Facing the Church.* New York: Paulist, 1975.

_____. *The Birth of the Messiah.* Garden City, NY: Doubleday, 1977.

Brown, R., K. Donfried, and J. Reumann, eds. *Peter in the New Testament: A Collaborative Assessment by Protestant and Roman Catholic Scholars.* Minneapolis: Augsburg/New York: Paulist, 1973.

Brown, Raymond E. and John P. Meier. *Antioch & Rome: New Testament Cradles of Christianity.* New York: Paulist, 1982.

Burger, C. "Jesu Täten nach Matthäus 8 und 9." *Zeitschrift für Theologie und Kirche* 70 (1973): 272-73.

Burnett, F.W. *The Testament of Jesus-Sophia: A Redaction-Critical Study of the Eschatological Discourse in Matthew.* Washington: University Press of America, 1981.

Butler, B.C. *The Originality of St. Matthew: A Critique of the Two-Document Hypothesis.* Cambridge: Cambridge University, 1951.

Carlston, Charles E. "Christology and Church in Matthew." In *The Four Gospels 1992: Festschrift Frans Neirynck,* ed. F. Van Segbroeck, C.M. Tuckett, G. Van Belle, and J. Verheyden. Volume II. Leuven: University Press, 1992, 1283-1304.

Carter, Warren. *What Are They Saying About Matthew's Sermon on the Mount?* New York: Paulist, 1994.

Cope, L. *Matthew: A Scribe Trained for the Kingdom of Heaven.* The Catholic Biblical Quarterly Monograph Series 5. Washington: Catholic Biblical Association of America, 1976.

Crosby, Michael H. *House of Disciples: Church, Economics & Justice in Matthew.* Maryknoll, NY: Orbis, 1988.

Davies, W.D. *The Sermon on the Mount.* Cambridge: Cambridge University, 1966.

_____. *The Setting of the Sermon on the Mount.* Cambridge: Cambridge University, 1964.

_____. "The Significance of the Law in Christianity." In *Christians and Jews,* ed. H. Küng and W. Kasper. Concilium. New York: Seabury, 1974, 24-32.

Davies, W.D. and Dale C. Allison, Jr. *Matthew.* International Critical Commentary. Edinburgh: T & T Clark, Vol. I. Matthew I-VII, 1988; Vol. II. Matthew VIII-XVIII, 1991.

Deutsch, C. *Hidden Wisdom and the Easy Yoke: Wisdom, Torah and Disciples in Matthew 11:25,30.* JSNT SS18. Sheffield: University of Sheffield Press, 1987.

_____. "Wisdom in Matthew: Transformation of a Symbol." *Novum Testamentum* 32 (1990): 13-47.

Dunn, James D.G. *Christology in the Making.* Philadelphia: Westminster, 1980.

Dupont, J. "Le point de vue de Matthieu dans le chapitre des paraboles." In *L'Évangile selon Matthieu: Rédaction et Théologie*, ed. M. Didier. Bibliotheca Ephemeridum Theologicarum Lovaniensium 29. Gembloux: Duculot, 1972, 221-60.

Edwards, Richard A. "Uncertain Faith: Matthew's Portrait of the Disciples." In *Discipleship in the New Testament*, ed. F. Segovia. Philadelphia: Fortress, 1985, 47-61.

Ellis, P.F. *Matthew: His Mind and His Message.* Collegeville: The Liturgical Press, 1974.

Farmer, William R. *The Synoptic Problem: A Critical Analysis.* New York: Macmillan, 1964; reprint, Dillsboro: Western North Carolina Press, 1976.

_____. *The Gospel of Jesus.* Louisville: Westminster/John Knox, 1994.

Fiorenza, Elisabeth Schüssler, ed. *Search the Scriptures: A Feminist Commentary.* Volume 2. New York: Crossroad, 1994.

France, R.T. *Matthew: Evangelist and Teacher.* Grand Rapids: Zondervan, 1989.

Frankemölle, H. *Jahwebund und Kirche Christi.* Neutestamentliche Abhandlungen 10. Münster: Aschendorff, 1974.

Gardner, Richard B. *Matthew.* Scottsdale, PA: Herald Press, 1991.

Garland, David E. *The Intention of Matthew 23.* Novum Testamentum Sup. 52. Leiden: Brill, 1979.

_____. *Reading Matthew: A Literary and Theological Commentary on the First Gospel.* New York: Crossroad, 1993.

Gerhardsson, B. *The Mighty Acts of Jesus According to Matthew.* Lund: CWK Gleerup, 1979.

Goulder, M.D. *Midrash and Lection in Matthew.* London: SPCK, 1974.

Guelich, Robert. *The Sermon on the Mount: A Foundation for Understanding.* Dallas: Word Publishing, 1982.

Gundry, Robert H. *The Use of the Old Testament in St. Matthew's Gospel with Special Reference to the Messianic Hope.* Supplements to Novum Testamentum 18. Leiden: E.J. Brill, 1967.

_____. *Matthew: A Commentary on His Literary and Theological Art.* Grand Rapids: Wm. B. Eerdmans, 1982 (second ed., 1994, *Matthew: A Commentary on His Handbook for a Mixed Church Under Persecution*).

Hagner, Donald A. *Matthew 1-13.* Word Biblical Commentary. Dallas: Word Publishing, 1993.

Hammerton-Kelly, R.G. "Attitudes to the Law in Matthew's Gospel: A Discussion of Matthew 5:18." *Biblical Research* 17 (1972): 19-32.

Hare, Douglas R.A. *The Theme of Jewish Persecution of Christians in the Gospel According to St. Matthew.* Society for New Testament Studies Monograph Series 6. Cambridge: Cambridge University, 1967.

_____. *The Son of Man Tradition.* Minneapolis: Fortress, 1990.

_____. *Matthew.* Interpretation. Louisville: John Knox, 1993.

Harrington, S.J., Daniel J. *The Gospel of Matthew.* Sacra Pagina. Collegeville: Liturgical Press, 1991.

Heil, John Paul. "Significant Aspects of the Healing Miracles in Matthew." *Catholic Biblical Quarterly* 41 (1979): 274-87.

_____. "The Narrative Structure of Matthew 27:55–28:20." *Journal of Biblical Literature* 110 (1991): 419-38.

_____. *The Death and Resurrection of Jesus: A Narrative-Critical Reading of Matthew 26-28.* Minneapolis: Augsburg Fortress, 1991.

Hill, David. "False Prophets and Charismatics: Structure and Interpretation in Matthew 7.15-23." *Biblica* 57 (1976): 327-48.

_____. "Son and Servant: An Essay on Matthean Christology." *Journal for the Study of the New Testament* 6 (1980): 2-16.

_____. "The Figure of Jesus in Matthew's Gospel: A Response to Professor Kingsbury's Literary-Critical Probe." *Journal for the Study of the New Testament* 21 (1984): 37-52.

Howell, David B. *Matthew's Inclusive Story. A Study in the Narrative Rhetoric of the First Gospel.* JSNTS 42. Sheffield: Sheffield Academic Press, 1990.

Hubbard, B.J. *The Matthean Redaction of a Primitive Apostolic Commissioning: An Exegesis of Matthew 28:16-20.* SBL Dissertation Series 19. Missoula: Society of Biblical Literature, 1974.

Hummel, R. *Die Auseinandersetzung zwischen Kirche und Judentum im Matthäusevangelium.* München: Kaiser Verlag, 1963.

Johnson, M.D. "Reflections on a Wisdom Approach to Matthew's Christology." *Catholic Biblical Quarterly* 36 (1974): 44-64.

Kilpatrick, G.D. *The Origins of the Gospel According to St. Matthew.* Oxford: Clarendon, 1946.

Kingsbury, Jack Dean. *The Parables of Jesus in Matthew 13: A Study in Redaction Criticism.* Richmond: John Knox, 1969.

_____. *Matthew: Structure, Christology, Kingdom.* Philadelphia: Fortress, 1975.

_____. "Observations on the Miracle Chapters of Matthew 8-9." *Catholic Biblical Quarterly* 40 (1978): 559-73.

_____. "The Figure of Peter in Matthew's Gospel as a Theological Problem." *Journal of Biblical Literature* 98 (1979): 67-83.

_____. *Jesus Christ in Matthew, Mark, and Luke*. Proclamation Commentaries. Philadelphia: Fortress, 1981.

_____. "The Figure of Jesus in Matthew's Story: A Rejoinder to David Hill." *Journal for the Study of the New Testament* 25 (1985): 61-81.

_____. *Matthew*. Rev. ed. Proclamation Commentaries. Philadelphia: Fortress, 1986.

_____. *Matthew as Story*. 2nd rev. ed. Philadelphia: Fortress, 1988.

_____. "Analysis of a Conversation." In *Social History of the Matthean Community*, ed. David L. Balch. Minneapolis: Augsburg Fortress, 1991, 259-63.

Kopas, Jane. "Jesus and Women in Matthew." *Theology Today* 47 (1990): 13-21.

Krentz, E. "The Extent of Matthew's Prologue: Toward the Structure of the First Gospel." *Journal of Biblical Literature* 83 (1964): 409-15.

Levine, Amy-Jill *The Social and Ethnic Dimensions of Matthean Salvation History. Go nowhere among the Gentiles... (Matt. 10:5b)*. Studies in the Bible and Early Christianity 14. Lewiston, NY: The Edwin Mellon Press, 1988.

Luz, Ulrich. "Die Jünger im Matthäusevangelium." *Zeitschrift für Neuentestamentliche Wissenschaft* 62 (1971): 141-71.

_____. *Matthew 1–7: A Continental Commentary*. Minneapolis: Augsburg Fortress, 1989.

Malina, Bruce J. and Jerome H. Neyrey. *Calling Jesus Names: The Social Value of Labels in Matthew*. Sonoma, CA: Polebridge Press, 1988.

Matera, Frank. "The Plot of Matthew's Gospel." *Catholic Biblical Quarterly* 49 (1987): 233-53.

Meier, John P. "Salvation-History in Matthew: In Search of a Starting Point." *Catholic Biblical Quarterly* 37 (1975): 203-15.

_____. *Law and History in Matthew's Gospel: A Redactional Study of Mt. 5:17-48.* Analecta Biblica 71. Rome: Biblical Institute, 1976.

_____. *The Vision of Matthew: Christ, Church and Morality in the First Gospel.* Theological Inquiries. New York: Paulist, 1979.

_____. *Matthew.* New Testament Message 3. Collegeville: Liturgical Press, 1981.

Minear, P. "The Disciples and Crowds in the Gospel of Matthew." *Anglican Theological Review.* Supplementary Series 3 (1974): 28.

Morris, Leon. *The Gospel According to Matthew.* Grand Rapids, MI: Wm. B. Eerdmans, 1992.

Nau, Arlo J. *Peter in Matthew: Discipleship, Diplomacy, and Dispraise.* Good News Studies 36. Collegeville, MN: Liturgical Press, 1992.

Neirynck, Frans. *Minor Agreements of Matthew and Luke Against Mark, with a Consultative List.* Bibliotheca Ephemeridum Theologicarum Lovaniensium 37. Louvain: Louvain University, 1974.

_____. *"Apo Tote Erkzato* and the Structure of Matthew." In *Evangelica II 1982-1991. Collected Essays by Frans Neirynck,* ed. F. Van Segbroeck. Leuven: University Press, 1991, 141-82. This article first appeared in *Ephemerides Theologicae Lovanienses* 64 (1988): 21-59.

_____. "Synoptic Problem." In *The New Jerome Biblical Commentary,* ed. R. Brown, S.S., J. Fitzmyer, S.J., and R. Murphy, O.Carm., 587-95. Englewood Cliffs, NJ: Prentice-Hall, 1990.

_____. "The Minor Agreements and Q." In *The Gospel Behind the Gospels: Current Studies on Q*, ed. Ronald A. Piper. Supplements to Novum Testamentum 75. Leiden: Brill, 1995, 49-72.

Nepper-Christensen, Poul. *Das Matthaüsevangelium. Ein judenchristliches Evangelium?* Åarhus: Universitetsforlaget, 1958.

Nolan, B.M. *The Royal Son of God: The Christology of Matthew 1-2 in the Setting of the Gospel.* Orbis Biblicus et Orientalis 23. Göttingen: Vandenhoeck & Ruprecht, 1979.

Orton, David E. *The Understanding Scribe: Matthew and the Apocalyptic Ideal.* JSNT SS25. Sheffield: University of Sheffield Press, 1989.

Overman, J. Andrew. *Matthew's Gospel and Formative Judaism: The Social World of the Matthean Community.* Minneapolis: Augsburg Fortress, 1990.

Perkins, Pheme. *Peter: Apostle for the Whole Church.* Columbia: University of South Carolina Press, 1994.

Pesch, W. *Matthäus der Seelsorger: Das neue Verständnis der Evangelien dargestellet am Beispiel von Matthäus 18.* Stuttgarter BibelStudien 2. Stuttgart: Katholisches Bibelwerk, 1966.

Powell, Mark Allan. "The Plot and Subplots of Matthew's Gospel." *New Testament Studies* 38 (1992): 187-204.

Przybylski, B. *Righteousness in Matthew and His World of Thought.* Society for New Testament Studies Monograph Series 41. Cambridge: Cambridge University, 1980.

Rothfuchs, W. *Die Erfüllungszitate des Matthäus-Evangeliums: Eine biblisch-theologische Untersuchung.* Beitrage zur Wissenschaft vom Alten und Neuen Testament 8. Stuttgart: W. Kohlhammer, 1969.

Saldarini, Anthony J. *Matthew's Christian-Jewish Community.* Chicago: University of Chicago, 1994.

Sand, A. *Das Evangelium nach Matthäus.* Regensburg: Friedrich Pustet, 1986.

_____. *Das Gesetz und die Propheten: Untersuchungen zur Theologie des Evangeliums nach Matthäus.* Biblische Untersuchungen 11. Regensburg: Friedrich Pustet, 1974.

Schaberg, Jane. *The Illegitimacy of Jesus.* San Francisco: Harper & Row, 1987.

Schweizer, E. "Observance of the Law and Charismatic Activity in Matthew." *New Testament Studies* 16 (1970): 213-30.

Senior, Donald. *The Passion Narrative According to Matthew: A Redactional Study.* Bibliotheca Ephemeridum Theologicarum Lovaniensium 39. Louvain: Louvain University, 1975.

_____. "The Death of Jesus and the Resurrection of the Holy Ones (Mt 27:51-53)." *Catholic Biblical Quarterly* 38 (1976): 312-29.

_____. "The Ministry of Continuity: Matthew's Gospel and the Intepretation of History." *The Bible Today* 82 (1976):670-76.

_____. *The Passion of Jesus in the Gospel of Matthew.* Passion Series 1. Collegeville, MN: Liturgical Press, 1985.

_____. "The Gospel of Matthew and Our Jewish Heritage." *The Bible Today* 27 (1989): 325-32.

_____. "The Jesus of Matthew." *Church* 5 (1989): 10-13.

_____. "Matthew's Account of the Burial of Jesus Mt 27,57-61." In *The Four Gospels 1992: Festschrift Frans Neirynck,* ed. F. Van Segbroeck, C.M. Tuckett, G. Van Belle, and J. Verheyden. Leuven: University Press, 1992, 1433-48.

Sheridan, M. "Disciples and Discipleship in Matthew and Luke." *Biblical Theology Bulletin* 3 (1973): 235-55.

Smith, Robert H. *Matthew*. Augsburg Commentary. Minneapolis: Augsburg, 1989.

Snodgrass, Klyne R. "Matthew's Understanding of the Law." *Interpretation* 46 (1992): 368-78.

Stanton, Graham N. , ed. *The Interpretation of Matthew*. Philadelphia: Fortress, 1983 (rev. ed., Edinburgh: T & T Clark, 1995).

_____. "The Communities of Matthew." *Interpretation* 46 (1992): 379-91.

_____. "The Origin and Purpose of Matthew's Gospel: Matthean Scholarship from 1945–1980." *Aufstieg und Neidergang der Romanischer Welt* II. 25.3 (1985): 1889-1951.

_____. *A Gospel for a New People: Studies in Matthew*. Edinburgh: T & T Clark, 1992.

Stark, Rodney. "Antioch as the Social Situation for Matthew's Gospel." In *Social History of the Matthean Community*, ed. D. Balch. Minneapolis: Augsburg Fortress, 1991, 189-210.

Stendahl, K. *The School of St. Matthew and Its Use of the Old Testament*. 1st American ed. Philadelphia: Fortress, 1968.

Stock, OSB, Augustine. *The Method and Message of Matthew*. Collegeville: Liturgical Press, 1994.

Strecker, G. *Der Weg der Gerechtigkeit: Untersuchung zur Theologie des Matthäus*. 2nd rev. ed. Göttingen: Vandenhoeck & Ruprecht, 1966.

_____. "Das Geschichtsverstandnis des Matthäus." *Evangelische Theologie* 26 (1966): 57-74; an English translation appeared in the *Journal of the American Academy of Religion* 35 (1967): 219-30.

Suggs, M.J. *Wisdom, Christology, and Law in Matthew's Gospel.* Cambridge: Harvard University, 1970.

Thompson, W.G. *Matthew's Advice to a Divided Community. Mt. 17,22–18,35.* Analecta Biblica 44. Rome: Biblical Institute, 1970.

_____. "Reflections on the Composition of Mt. 8:1-9:34." *Catholic Biblical Quarterly* 33 (1971): 365-388.

_____. "An Historical Perspective in the Gospel of Matthew." *Journal of Biblical Literature* 93 (1974): 244.

Tilborg, Sjef Van. *The Jewish Leaders in Matthew.* Leiden: Brill, 1972.

Trilling, Wolfgang. *Das Wahre Israel: Studien zur Theologie des Matthäus Evangeliums.* STANT 10. 3rd rev. ed. München: Kösel-Verlag, 1964.

Van Segbroeck, F. "Les citations d'accomplissement dans l'Évangile selon Matthieu d'après trois ouvrages récents." In *L'Évangile selon Matthieu: Rédaction et Théologie,* ed. M. Didier, 107-30. Bibliotheca Ephemeridum Theologicarum Lovaniensium 29. Gembloux: Duculot, 1972.

Van Tilborg, S. *The Jewish Leaders in Matthew.* Leiden: E.J. Brill, 1972.

Verseput, D. "The Role and Meaning of the Son of God Title in Matthew's Gospel." *New Testament Studies* 33 (1987): 532-56.

Viviano, O.P., Benedict T. "Where Was the Gospel According to Matthew Written?" *Catholic Biblical Quarterly* 41 (1979): 533-46.

_____. "The Gospel According to Matthew." In *The New Jerome Biblical Commentary,* ed. Raymond Brown, S.S., Joseph Fitzmyer, S.J., and Roland E. Murphy, O.Carm. Englewood Cliffs, NJ: Prentice-Hall, 1990.

Wainwright, Elaine Mary. *Toward a Feminist Critical Reading of The Gospel According to Matthew.* BZNT 60. Berlin/New York: Walter de Gruyter, 1991.

Walker, Rolf. *Die Heilsgeschichte im ersten Evangelium.* Göttingen: Vandenhoeck & Ruprecht, 1967.

Wilkins, Michael J. *The Concept of Disciple in Matthew's Gospel: As Reflected in the Use of the Term* Mathetes. Supplements to Novum Testamentum 59. Leiden: E.J. Brill, 1988.

Wire, Antoinette Clark. "Gender Roles in a Scribal Community." In *Social History of the Matthean Community*, ed. D. Balch. Minneapolis: Augsburg Fortress, 1991, 87-121.

Zumstein, J. *La Condition du Croyant dans L Évangile selon Matthieu.* Orbis Biblicus et Orientalis 16. Göttingen: Vandenhoeck & Ruprecht, 1977.

Other Books in This Series

What are they saying about the Prophets?
by David P. Reid, SS. CC.

What are they saying about Moral Norms?
by Richard M. Gula, S.S.

What are they saying about Sexual Morality?
by James P. Hanigan

What are they saying about Dogma?
by William E. Reiser, S.J.

What are they saying about Peace and War?
by Thomas A. Shannon

What are they saying about Papal Primacy?
by J. Michael Miller, C.S.B.

What are they saying about Matthew?
by Donald Senior, C.P.

What are they saying about Matthew's Sermon on the Mount?
by Warren Carter

What are they saying about Biblical Archaeology?
by Leslie J. Hoppe, O.F.M.

What are they saying about Theological Method?
by J.J. Mueller, S.J.

What are they saying about Virtue?
by Anthony J. Tambasco

What are they saying about Genetic Engineering?
by Thomas A. Shannon

What are they saying about Salvation?
by Rev. Denis Edwards

What are they saying about Mark?
by Frank J. Matera

What are they saying about Luke?
by Mark Allan Powell

What are they saying about John?
by Gerard S. Sloyan

What are they saying about Acts?
by Mark Allan Powell

What are they saying about the Ministerial Priesthood?
by Rev. Daniel Donovan